THE
BEAVER
AND THE
DRAGON

How China Out-Manoeuvred Canada's
Diplomacy, Security, and Sovereignty

CHARLES BURTON

EDITED BY Kevin Cavanagh

The Beaver and the Dragon © Ottawa, 2025 Charles Burton

First Edition published in Canada
Published by Optimum Publishing International

All rights reserved. No part of this publication may be reproduced in any form or by any means whatsoever without permission in writing from the publisher, except by a reviewer who may quote passages of customary brevity.

Library and Archives Canada Cataloguing in Publication
Title: The Beaver and the Dragon, How China Out-Manoeuvred Canada's Diplomacy, Security, and Sovereignty

Subjects: National Security, Canada-China Relations, Diplomacy, Statecraft, Foreign Affairs and Policy
Description: Optimum Publishing International, Canada edition
ISBN 978-0-88890-371-6 Trade Paperback

Printed and bound in Canada.
Marquis Printing

For information on rights or any submissions, please e-mail to
Optimum: deanb@opibooks.com
Optimum Publishing International
Dean Baxendale, President & CEO
Toronto, Canada

www.optimumpublishinginternational.com
www.opibooks.com
Twitter @opibooks | Instagram @opibooks

Contents

About the contributors	vii
Introduction by the Publisher	ix
Preface	xiii
One night in Shanghai	1
Canada's bumpy journey with China	6
The media lens	21
The Stephen Harper Era	**23**
A more sophisticated engagement with China	25
Economic titan China needs to act like a leader	29
Farewell, Mr. Lai	33
Harper in China: Juggling oil sales and core principles	37
Stephen Harper's new trade rules safeguard Canada's interests	41
Why did Harper go to China? The ethnic vote. And money	44
Bending over backward for Beijing	48
More than empty rhetoric as China engages in Communist democracy	51
Taking stock of the Chinese stock market slide	54
China learns it can't control the laws of economics	57
Who will march with China at Xi's parade?	61
Relations with China should hinge on more than short-term economic value	64
Goodbye to the age of China's 'little emperors'	68
The Justin Trudeau Era	**73**
Trudeau's dance with the dragon: China must give as much as it takes	75
Trade with China never comes free	79
Visit to China a tricky one for Trudeau	82
Enlisting Beijing to help stop fentanyl exports won't be easy	85
Hong Kong, and the litany of Beijing's betrayal	88

Oh Canada: The roaring silence around trade talks with China	91
As Xi sets his sights on the world, the ruse is dispensed with	95
Does Trudeau really believe trade with China is 'free'?	98
Canada-China relations are now ripe for a rethink	102
A red flag for Canada after the Putinization of Xi's dictatorship	105
Canada caught in the crossfire of the U.S.-China trade war	108
China threatens and intimidates people within Canada as Ottawa remains silent	111
Canada takes note as China gets tough with Australia	114
Canada needs a foreign agent registry to help it tackle China's influence	117
In Canadian universities, China's espionage is hiding in plain sight	120
Canada looks on as Biden rallies other allies to counter China	123
Time to wake up and take megalomaniacs seriously	126
China's growing economic angst is another political threat for Xi	129
At last, Canada is confronting the problem of foreign influence	132
Here's how China turns our politicians into pawns	135

Hostage diplomacy 139

Canadians detained in China are pawns in a bigger geopolitical game	141
Garratt's release a win for Canada — and China	144
A thorny path lies ahead for Canadian-Chinese relations	148
Canada must develop a backbone in its dealings with China	152
China-Canada tensions are no passing storm	156
In Canada, the tide of opinion is turning on China	159
Kovrig and Spavor's two-year ordeal and what it means for Canada–China relations	162
Treatment of the Two Michaels reveals Canada's lack of leverage in Beijing	165

Huawei and Canada's 5G security 169

Weighing Huawei in Canada-China relations	171
Why Canada can't let Huawei build a 5G network	175
Canada must boost its security apparatus against China and Russia	178

The Coronavirus   *183*

Many concerns as Canadians wait for evacuation from China   *185*

Beijing's coronavirus bungling makes Canada's choice on Huawei even easier   *188*

Holding China to account for the COVID-19 coverup   *191*

Canada's sovereignty vs China and Trump   *197*

As Trump roils, Ottawa shuffles the deck to play a new China card   *199*

How Xi trumped Trump at the G20 summit   *202*

Why are Chinese police operating in Canada, while our own government and security services apparently look the other way?   *205*

What is Ottawa doing to protect Canada's sovereignty against China?   *209*

Canada's new top soldier needs to protect our Arctic from China   *212*

As Canada scrambles for options, beware the temptation of China   *215*

Donald Trump has extreme designs on Canada: Here is what he really wants   *218*

China weaponizes death penalty as relations with Canada deteriorate   *221*

Donald Trump is helping Xi Jinping achieve his grand vision for China   *224*

Canada in trade wars with the superpowers — with no room for error   *227*

New evidence indicates China's Communist Party is reining in strongman Xi Jinping   *230*

Is China a better trading partner than Trump's America?   *233*

Hope for the future   *237*

Index   *241*

About the author: from student to diplomat

CHARLES BURTON IS A CANADIAN-BASED SINOLOGIST whose perceptions help government policymakers understand contemporary China, its calculating foreign relations, and its evolution from Chairman Mao's isolated, backward "Red China" to today's modern, unbending superpower.

Burton has spent years working, studying and travelling in China. As a student, he became fluent in Mandarin at Cambridge University in the UK, then attended Shanghai's Fudan University, the lone westerner in a communal dorm room, immersed in the study of ancient Chinese thought.

He went on to become a Political Science professor in Canada and a diplomat at Canada's embassy in Beijing, constantly exploring both ancient, texturous Confucian philosophy and bare-knuckle 21st-century Chinese politics. Today he is a senior fellow at Sinopsis.cz, a China-focused think tank based in Prague.

Burton's bilingualism enables him to scrutinize the subtleties of untranslated Party announcements or state-controlled media reports, but he also developed an innate sense of China's national character through years of living among and engaging with neighbours and friends in Chinese cities.

Over the past 20 years he has written over two hundred opinion pieces for Canadian and international news media and dozens of scholarly articles and reports for governments and think tanks. He does several hundred media interviews for print, radio and TV yearly. Western bureaucrats and politicians have quietly acknowledged his insights as priority reading. In telling the story of how he came to become an international China expert, this book uses a selection of his media articles to examine how the world has been changing before our eyes, and how an authoritarian regime plans and pursues global dominance.

Written in real time — seeing and chronicling historical shifts as they happened — these essays are a clear-eyed look at how Canada and other nations have spent decades (and billions of dollars) imploring China to recast itself alongside liberalized nations guided by democratic values, fair commerce and respect for human rights.

But while numerous nations tried to turn the emerging giant into a lucrative economic and diplomatic partner, China ended up being the one that was shaping the world to its liking, and in the process applying its own values to the concepts of global diplomacy and justice.

About the editor

THIS BOOK WAS EDITED BY KEVIN CAVANAGH, who spent 35 years as a reporter, editor and opinion writer at Canadian newspapers including the *National Post*, *Hamilton Spectator* and *St. Catharines Standard*. He was a Visiting Journalist Fellow at University of Oxford (UK), a Commonwealth Press Union Journalism Fellow, and won the CIJ Award for Outstanding Investigative Reporting in Canada.

Introduction by the Publisher

IN THE WORLD OF INTELLIGENCE AND national security, few moments are more frustrating than when patterns are clear, the threat is evident, and yet the warning goes unheeded. This book, *The Beaver and the Dragon*, is a record of precisely that kind of moment — extended over twenty years. It captures, in stark and compelling form, a chronicle of warnings that Canada chose to ignore, soften, or postpone. It offers readers a view not only into the nature of the Chinese Communist Party (CCP) and its influence operations, but also into the troubling weaknesses in Canada's political and institutional responses to them.

Charles Burton has long stood apart in the national conversation about China. His credentials are rare: a sinologist trained in classical and modern Chinese political thought; a fluent Mandarin speaker; a Canadian diplomat who served in Beijing; and a political scientist with decades of study into the ideology, structure, and motivations of the CCP. But what makes Burton unique is not merely his academic or diplomatic resume. It is his courage to name uncomfortable truths and his capacity to see clearly what many chose to rationalize away.

From the earliest essays in this volume, written in the wake of the 2008 Beijing Olympics, Burton identified a shift: China was no longer seeking integration into a liberal international order. It was adapting that order to serve its own authoritarian goals. Where many Canadian policymakers saw opportunity, Burton saw ideological and geopolitical risk. He foresaw the consequences of deepening economic entanglement without political clarity. He observed — long before it became common knowledge — how the United Front Work Department and its proxy organizations operated with impunity in Canada, how the diaspora was being surveilled, manipulated and oppressed, and how Canadian institutions from the municipal to the federal level were being quietly co-opted to serve the needs of Beijing.

For those of you who served in intelligence and security roles, much of what Charles wrote aligned with internal threat assessments, many of which never saw the light of day, but some did. From controversial intelligence reports like Sidewinder (CSIS, 1999) to, two recent public inquiries one in British Columbia better knows as the Cullen Commission (2023) and The Hogue Inquiry (2025, Foreign Interference Commission) all spoke to the observations that Burton had been making for years. Many Canadian investigative journalists and Chinese diaspora members and organizations have also contributed significant volumes of research, media stories and expert testimony to parliament that clearly demonstrated the intentions and objectives of the Chinese Communist Party within Canada and more broadly, their global objectives. Burton understood these insights and through his original columns he articulated it publicly, consistently, and with a moral urgency that should have been hard to ignore.

This book is not just a collection of essays. It is a longitudinal study of Canadian strategic drift. Burton methodically charts how successive governments from Chrétien through Harper to Trudeau failed to develop a coherent policy on China that served our long-term strategic interests. He shows how, under the guise of economic diplomacy and multicultural outreach, critical scrutiny was abandoned. In some cases, Chinese state interests were prioritized over Canadian democratic norms and the security of our own citizens. Politicians seemingly under the sphere of influence of Beijing abandoned hard-won principles for engaging authoritarian states who do not share the collective principles of freedom under a democratic governance model.

INTRODUCTION BY THE PUBLISHER

When the People's Republic of China detained two Canadians in retaliation for the arrest of Huawei CFO Meng Wanzhou, the moment was not an aberration. It was the culmination of years of misunderstanding the CCP's worldview. Charles Burton understood this well. He understood that this was not a misunderstanding between trading partners. It was strategic statecraft — and Canada was unprepared.

What distinguishes this book from others in the genre, is its fusion of lived insight, historical perspective, and predictive accuracy. Burton does not simply catalogue events. He explains why they happened, what ideological forces drive them, and how Canada's domestic vulnerabilities made those outcomes possible. In this, This book becomes both a witness statement and a policy guide.

Burton also captures what many inside government feared to say publicly: that Canada's institutions — our courts, our universities, our political parties, and even elements of our media — have been vulnerable to manipulation. Not always out of malice, but often due to complacency or the naive belief that engagement alone could moderate authoritarian intent.

What makes his analysis more urgent is that these are not static threats. The CCP has grown more sophisticated, more assertive, and more willing to use grey-zone tactics to achieve its goals. Influence operations, cyber intrusions, economic coercion, and disinformation campaigns are now part of a seamless strategy aimed at weakening liberal democracies from within. Burton's work provides an interpretive lens that is indispensable to understanding these threats not just in Canada, but across allied nations.

I want to emphasize that Burton's work does not come from a place of hostility toward China as a civilization or its people. Quite the opposite. His respect for the depth of Chinese history and philosophy informs his deep concern for how the Chinese Communist Party uses those traditions as instruments of control. His has a principled stand against authoritarianism, not against a nation or its culture.

The final section of the book, "Hopes for the Future," is perhaps the most important. It reminds us that clarity is not cynicism, and that vigilance is not paranoia. Burton offers a path forward that balances strategic realism with democratic values. He makes clear that engagement must be based on reciprocity, transparency, and an unflinching commitment to our own principles.

To ignore the insights in this book is to repeat the mistakes of the past. To read it seriously is to begin the hard work of national renewal. Charles Burton has done this country a great service by documenting what so many refused to confront. It is now up to policymakers, security professionals, academics, and citizens to ensure that this service was not in vain.

Dean Baxendale
Publisher, Optimum Publishing International

Preface

From over 200 articles that Charles Burton has published in the news media examining China's complex relationship with Canada and the west, this 2020 essay gave readers a particularly clear sense of the challenges that governments and agencies face when dealing with the regime in Beijing. Written at a time when COVID-19 was on its way to killing millions around the world, and when Canadians Michael Kovrig and Michael Spavor were innocent political hostages in Chinese jails, this analysis drew a searing rebuke from the Chinese Embassy in Ottawa.

The Chinese Communist Party is not really very Chinese at all

(PUBLISHED 3 JULY 2020 IN *THE GLOBE AND MAIL*)

THE WAY THE CHINESE COMMUNIST PARTY depicts it, rising tensions between China and the West are due to a declining Western civilization, led by the United States, attempting to beat back the inevitable rise of China. We are assured that Chinese culturally-based non-liberal ideologies and non-democratic institutions offer great promise for future global prosperity and justice under Chinese leadership.

But as someone who has lived his life between China and Canada, I am deeply troubled by the prediction of inevitability of a winner-takes-all clash of superpowers starting very soon. Are there really no universal values to bind us in our common humanity, as Chinese President Xi Jinping insists there are not?

If Mr. Xi is so confident in the superiority of his repressive program of "socialism with Chinese characteristics," why is there so much secrecy, brutal suppression of political debate and digital censorship in his domestic and international policies? Why is there so much dissembling and disinformation in his regime's engagement with Western governments and the public?

For example, he suggests there is "clear" and "solid" evidence that both Michael Kovrig and Michael Spavor are spies (for Canada?). Falsely claiming that their arrest is neither arbitrary nor politically motivated on the one hand, while on the other unable to provide anything that suggests different, and urging that the Canadian media and politicians cease pressuring them on these points with our "megaphone diplomacy," seems such a feeble and pitiful approach, and frankly, not very Chinese.

In the late 1970s, I was honoured to be the first foreign student admitted to the history of ancient Chinese thought program, in the department of philosophy at Shanghai's Fudan University, since the 1960 Sino-Soviet split. All my professors had just recently returned to campus after years of imprisonment and forced labour in the Communist Party's Great Proletarian Cultural Revolution.

With enormous good grace, considering the circumstances, my kindly and generous teachers readily took me in as one of their own. What they taught me was that China's cultural greatness yesterday, today and tomorrow lies in the immutable principles clearly and simply expressed in the classical Chinese of the ancient sages of China's Confucian tradition.

I learned that honesty and integrity are the most important traits that Confucius repeatedly emphasizes throughout his *Analects*. In his discourse on honesty, Confucius stresses how being sincere gives individuals the integrity necessary to make progress along the way: "Be sincere and true to your word, serious and careful in your actions; and you will get along even among barbarians. But if you are not sincere and untrustworthy in your speech, frivolous and careless in your actions, how will you get along even among your own neighbours?"

But what we get out of the Chinese Communist Party today is dishonesty and insincerity. Kevin and Julia Garratt, who were brutally held for almost two years from 2014, and like Mr. Kovrig and Mr. Spavor also falsely charged with ill-defined espionage crimes, were also just innocent pawns in the Communist Party's pathetic and contemptible hostage diplomacy.

There is no valid reason to bar Canadian canola seed or wood imports into China. They just made it up. Prison camp facilities holding huge numbers of Uyghurs in Xinjiang are an appalling violation of human decency amounting to cultural genocide and nothing else.

COVID-19 was not brought to Wuhan by U.S. forces participating in the Military World Games last fall, as Chinese foreign ministry spokesman Zhao Lijian alleged. And the National Security Law for Hong Kong is simply a betrayal of China's commitment to maintain Hong Kong's freedom and rule of law until 2047.

These are the indisputable facts of these matters. The alternative narratives coming out of Beijing are unconscionable, perfidious bafflegab.

If the party seeks to devastate the international rules-based order, then be transparent and open about it. It is a betrayal to claim the party's dissembling is true to Chinese cultural imperatives. In this sense, the Chinese Communist Party is ultimately not very Chinese.

My respected Fudan professors are all gone now, their lives shortened by the torture and political persecution they suffered in the 1960s and 1970s. But I am confident that if they were still around to mentor their unpresuming Canadian student, they would tell me that liberal democracy and defence of human dignity is actually the true Confucian Way in this modern age.

One night in Shanghai

I'VE TRAVELLED TO CHINA 70 TIMES OR MORE — as a student, a diplomat, a program administrator and just a visitor — collectively spending years of my life there. But something about this trip seemed different before I even left Canada.

It's a hot, sticky day in August 2018 and after a month travelling in China, I go home tomorrow. I'm in the massive, bustling port city of Shanghai which, at 30 million people, is more than three times the size of New York City. It has three-quarters of Canada's entire population.

Forty years ago I was a student here at Fudan University. The Shanghai I knew then was a different world. Nothing was modern, there were no skyscrapers, streets usually had more bicycles than cars.

Today people get around on a world-class metro system with 20 different lines and 800 kilometres of track, or drive on a remarkable network of elevated highways. Towering contemporary architecture defines the famous skyline. Each year more than three million foreign tourists come to walk Shanghai's waterfront, explore museums, experience ancient temples, savour the food.

As for this tourist, I would spend the final day of my trip visiting old friends and classmates, including Tao Liming, my dear friend and university roommate who was in the late stages of cancer.

Tao's spacious, modern highrise was a stark contrast to the humble housing he lived in years before, with one main room open to the sidewalk and the bedroom in a loft. In those days there was no toilet, so one used the public facility down the street, and went to the local bathhouse to shower (charge was 15 Chinese cents).

Tao was at his best early in the day, so I left the Fudan guesthouse before 6 am in a Didi Chuxing, which is China's convenient equivalent of an Uber. At his apartment Tao was weak but in good spirits and very pleased that I had come. We had a wonderful reunion, re-lived special stories, took photos. Our parting was truly sad; he passed away not long after my visit.

Next I had coffee with Canada's Consul-General in Shanghai, Weldon Epp, with whom I'd served at the Embassy in Beijing in the late 1990s.

Then it was off to lunch with about 15 of my old Fudan friends. While many of our classmates now had various government positions in Beijing, these Shanghai natives had managed to get posts that kept them working locally.

The last stop was with my old Professor Wang Zhemin, another meaningful visit that ended with dinner at a restaurant next door to his apartment.

Reflecting on a special day and thinking about tomorrow's flight home, I strolled back to the hotel around 9 p.m.

Standing by the front door were two agents from China's Ministry of State Security. They had been waiting 13 hours for me to return, and were not pleased. They wanted me to answer some questions. Given the late hour, rather than go to a Ministry compound, they said we would start the interrogation in an empty room at the guesthouse.

It was like something out of John le Carré. In all my travels to China I'd never experienced anything like this, but in hindsight perhaps it shouldn't have been completely unexpected.

Before leaving Canada, my visa application — a routine I'd done many times — was for some reason denied by Chinese authorities. But then a few days later I received a call saying if I took my passport to the Chinese visa centre in Toronto, a visa would be issued. When I picked it up, instead of the usual three months, I was allowed just 30 days. No explanation given.

And now, at the end of my trip, I'm sitting in a Shanghai hotel room across from a Chinese state security agent. His colleague stayed between me and the door. A third man was out in the hall.

Bizarrely, much of their questioning focused on Yan Beiming, my professor of ancient Chinese philosophy back at Fudan University. He died in 1990.

During the 1960s Cultural Revolution, Chairman Mao Zedong unleashed the Red Guard to persecute anyone — government officials, military officers, academics — who was deemed a threat to his hardline doctrine. Professor Yan was targeted because he was a scholar of Confucian and Buddhist philosophy. Decades earlier, after China's humiliation in the 1919 Treaty of Versailles, he'd been a prominent voice in national debates over political reform vs continued Confucianism.

But that was long ago. On this night in the Fudan guesthouse, we were going on at length about my links to a man who had been dead nearly 30 years.

Speaking in Mandarin, the senior man read aloud from a file. They had a remarkable amount of information about me. For instance, they'd obviously had people taking notes during my Chinese Politics lectures back at Brock University. As well, someone from the university's (now defunct) Confucius Institute was aware of my involvement with a discussion group of Beijing scholars about the significance of Taoist thought, and had reported this to the Chinese Consulate in Toronto.

Evidently the Security Ministry was concerned that, since I'd once been Professor Yan's student, my own views of Taoism as a potential basis for democracy in China meant I was sustaining a long-dead scholar's perceived threat to communism — I was a challenge to President Xi Jinping's authority as supreme emperor-like autocrat. It seemed crazy.

This line of questioning went on for hour after sleep-deprived hour. My inquisitors never resorted to violence or anger (even when I contested their discourses that defended the Communist regime). Yet more than once, with the menacing tone of a threat, they said I would soon be moved elsewhere for further questioning. I couldn't help but think that wherever I went next would not be as comfortable as the hotel room.

Then something changed. At some point before dawn, my interrogators left the room. (Earlier on, I had mentioned as casually as possible that a couple of my old university classmates were now senior officials in Beijing. I could see this caught the agents' attention.)

Five minutes passed, then 15, then 20. Nobody returned. I peered out of the doorway — the hall was empty. Heart racing, I grabbed my small shoulder bag, passport and phone, but didn't switch on the phone. I did not go to my room to pack my large suitcase, just went straight down several flights of stairs and left the property through a back gate, where I was shown into a car waiting on the roadside.

Google says it's a 37-minute drive from the guesthouse to Shanghai's sprawling Pudong Airport, but it felt much longer. Concerned we would be pursued, I constantly looked out the rear window to see if anyone was following us. Of course, everyone on the highway was following us — we were all going the same way! All the while, the woman driver chatted away in heavily Shanghai-accented Mandarin.

At the airport I was met by two young women at the curb on the departures level. They led me inside and down some stairs to a windowless room, which had a Thermos bottle of hot water, some instant coffee, powdered creamer and a few biscuits in plastic packages. I waited there alone for some time, then was taken through service corridors to a first-class passenger lounge, where nice food was brought to me as I sat in a corner as discreetly as possible.

Next I was led to a car. In China it is normal for VIPs or business leaders to be chauffeured from the first-class lounge to their waiting planes. No crowded shuttle buses for them.

Driving across the busy tarmac, past baggage wagons and fuel trucks, we stopped beside an airliner with its engines running. I hustled out of the car, up the boarding stairs and into the crowded cabin moments before it began to taxi out for takeoff. We were soon airborne. My head was spinning.

Two hours later the tires chirped as the jet touched down in Seoul, South Korea. I could finally exhale, but I only really calmed down the next day when I landed in Toronto.

I had many questions about what happened. Why had the authorities waited until I'd been in China for a month before making their move? It turns out they had planned to track me through my Chinese phone, but unfortunately for them I never used it. And apparently none of those facial recognition security cameras I walked past for weeks alerted them to where I was.

The Security Ministry only located me after the Fudan guesthouse registered my stay with the police, entering my passport into the state system. (When staying with various friends earlier in the trip, we hadn't bothered with the legally required but typically ignored visit to the local police station to fill out a temporary household registration form.)

Whoever arranged my passage through Shanghai airport, getting me into the first-class lounge meant that I did not have to pass through customs, where my passport would have been scanned and my presence detected.

After I got back to Canada, the Security Ministry sent me WeChat messages (in Chinese) expressing dismay that I had left. Reading those texts, it's clear they tried, and failed, to locate me at the airport.

Some day I hope to go back to find out how this was done and thank those who got me out of a very sticky situation.

Canada's bumpy journey with China

WHEN I FIRST TRAVELLED THERE IN the 1970s to study its ancient philosophy, China was poor and weak and isolated. It played no significant role in global affairs. The policies of the Chinese Communist Party (CCP), Mao Zedong's thinking, and the ideology of proletarian revolution were not of much interest to Canadians or to Canada's domestic or foreign affairs.

That has of course changed dramatically. As China became less secluded in the late 20th century, Canada and other countries reached out to pursue diplomatic ties, intellectual partnerships, tourism opportunities and billions of dollars' worth of commerce.

Over the past 50 years there has been much navigating of societal and cultural differences, the tenor of Canada-China relations ranging from hopeful optimism to deep-freeze hostility. Along the way have been many teachable moments for all concerned.

In my own career I became intimately familiar with China personally and professionally, learning its language, knowing its people, absorbing its philosophy, observing its politics.

As a sinologist and a writer, I have in the past two decades published more than 200 newspaper articles that observe high-profile milestones and flashpoints, but also the nuances, complexities and tensions of China's relations with the west.

As a basis for reviewing China's rise and its global role in the modern era, this book revisits a cross-section of those newspaper columns spanning a very eventful era from 2009 to 2025.

My own interest in China, however, goes back much further.

CANADA'S BUMPY JOURNEY WITH CHINA

In 1969, when I was a Grade 9 student, a bookshop opened on Rideau Street, halfway between my school and our family home. I often stopped in to break up my long walk home, especially in the depths of an Ottawa winter.

Progressive Books was unlike any store I'd ever seen. Images of Chairman Mao were prominent.

All the books were from China, but printed in English and other languages. And they were cheap! I still have my *Constitution of the People's Republic of China* in a red plastic cover with golden letters, which cost 15 cents.

I bought magazines like *China Reconstructs*, *China Pictorial*, *Chinese Literature*, the weekly *Peking Review*, and the *Selected Works of Mao Tsetung*. Reading them cover to cover on weekends and after school, these materials were a world of different ideas. Previously I knew little about Marx, Engels, Lenin and Stalin, but now I was reading that Soviet hegemonism was a threat to world peace, the "new tsars" had betrayed the world revolution, and Canada's leaders were the "running dogs" of U.S.-led western imperialism. (I got the message: Soviet Russians and American monopolistic capitalists, equally bad.)

There never seemed to be any other customers in the store. Presumably Communist authorities funded it and sent the reading materials from China. At the time there was no People's Republic of China (PRC) embassy in Ottawa, as Canada still recognized Chiang Kai-shek's régime, exiled in Taiwan, as China's legitimate government.

The staff looked gaunt and wore threadbare clothes, but were friendly. They told me they were members of the Communist Party, and asked if I would organize a Marxist cell of students at my school, to foment a transformation in Canada to support Chairman Mao's intended world revolution. They even explained how to go about doing this. I didn't believe this was all that feasible, and besides I was already busy as president of the Latin Club and singing in the choir down at the Cathedral.

Eventually Progressive Books went out of business, and I got on with completing high school. But my fascination with China persisted.

As a University of Toronto undergrad, I was captivated by a politics course called "Modern China in Revolution", especially classes on Chinese "religion" — Confucianism, Taoism, and Chinese Buddhist Philosophy. My professor noticed my interest and inspired me to go on to Cambridge University, and its Oriental Studies program.

Arriving in the UK shortly after the death of Chairman Mao, at Cambridge I began learning to speak and read Chinese. This opened a whole new sense of understanding and, riveted by China's dramatic power vacuum left by Mao's demise, I often went into London to visit Chinese booksellers.

For its commemorative funeral edition, *China Pictorial* blurred any photos of the pernicious Gang of Four, senior members of a radical political elite (one of them was Mao's widow) who were now being prosecuted for implementing Mao's harsh policies.

Closely following the Gang of Four's trial and the arcane politicized rationale behind it, I realized that Chinese-language accounts were much more lively and clearer than the turgid English-translated propaganda I'd been reading since I was a teenager. As my command of Mandarin continued to grow, I decided I would be better off continuing my studies in China. I applied to the Canada-China Scholars Exchange Program, and was accepted to study ancient Chinese philosophy at Fudan University.

I arrived in China at a good moment, historically speaking. After 10 years of fear and distrust during the Cultural Revolution, my cohort at Fudan was the first to be selected based on competitive entrance exams. These would be the most formative and fascinating years of my life.

Life in dorm Building Four meant being in close company with earnest students 24/7, sharing the same space, eating the same food. None of my roommates had ever had contact with any non-Chinese before meeting me, but we got on well and they adjusted to my cultural differences. Their only request was that I wear Chinese clothes, so I acquired a Mao jacket.

I was welcomed without reservation to assimilate into their society. In Chinese culture, this means an unbreakable friendship for life and an iron obligation to loyalty. Some of my dorm mates became senior officials in the Communist régime while others emigrated to the U.S., but to this day the bond of our shared past overcomes all.

―――

My most important discovery at Fudan involved the perils of assuming that linguistic translations capture the accurate meaning of original text that was not just written in another language but in another culture.

At Cambridge I'd read the Chinese classics in dual-language editions, the English version having been translated by James Legge. At Fudan I was given an annotated copy of the *Analects of Confucius* in the original Chinese, and told to read it. I quickly detected that the Chinese-language introduction differed greatly from what I had read in English translation. Quite impressed by my powers of shrewd observation, I felt every bit the savvy modern 1970s *sinologue,* a budding Confucian intellectual already familiar with the ancient wisdom by having read its English translations.

Sitting in that Shanghai dorm, dressed in my Mao suit and cloth shoes — my copy of the Legge translation at hand, as well as F.S. Couvreur's *Dictionnaire Classique de la Langue Chinoise* — I prepared for an afternoon of gratified reading.

It was anything but.

The Analects were not unfolding smoothly at all. As I kept reading, I felt a knot of intellectual unease, and in the confines of our dorm my anxiety became palpable. Finally one of my roommates asked if there was anything the matter. As realization set in, I said in angst, "I've got it all wrong! I have completely misunderstood Confucius!"

The fact that this westerner had been misinterpreting Confucius was hardly news to my roommates. For me, however, it was a eureka moment in reverse.

I came to realize that my non-Chinese readings of Confucius were shaped by an underlying bias in translations by Legge — a Presbyterian Scot — compounded by my reliance on the *Dictionnaire Classique de la langue Chinoise* by Couvreur — a French Jesuit. Unfortunately my Cambridge tutors had not corrected (or perhaps even noticed) the fact I was mangling the meaning of Confucius due to reading him in translation.

This was a case of Chinese philosophical thought being interpreted through an English language Judeo-Christian lens. Since that watershed moment I have often realized there are many things expressed in Chinese that cannot be identically stated in English, and vice versa. I also accept that Chinese people, ancient and modern, have quite a different life of the mind to my own.

These would be important lessons for me in the years to come.

Completing my Fudan studies in 1980 and returning to Canada, the next few years were eclectic.

In 1981 I took a job with the Department of National Defence, who trained me to read Russian. Military "listeners" in Canada's high Arctic would intercept Soviet communications in Cyrillic and send them to me. I read them and wrote reports (in English) of anything deemed of interest. (I was struck by the paradox that, as I sat in an Ottawa office translating these posts, Russian diplomats would each day be parking their cars in Vincent Massey Park just across the street.)

The following year I returned to the University of Toronto to do a PhD, writing my thesis on post-Mao ideology. In 1987 I joined the Association of University and Colleges of Canada to administer a program which funded exchanges between 20 Canadian and 20 Chinese universities for collaborative research and technology transfer.

———

In 1989 I became a professor of Political Science at Brock University in St. Catharines, Ontario. This was precisely when China was beset by unprecedented student protests demanding democratic reforms from the Communist government. As the standoff intensified between the protesting students and the regime in Beijing, foreign correspondents covered the growing drama and a global audience was intrigued to see thousands of students demanding open, accountable governance from an authoritarian regime.

The dream about a new era for China ended in early June when columns of tanks brutally crushed throngs of pro-democracy protesters in the bloody Tiananmen Square massacre. One of the backers of the protests, Wang Zhaojun, had been my roommate at Fudan University. After the crackdown he fled China, crossed the Pacific and for a time lived with me as a Tiananmen exile in a quiet Canadian neighbourhood.

During my career at Brock, on two occasions the university gave me leaves of absence so I could serve diplomatic postings at Canada's embassy in China. When Canada opened its first Beijing embassy back in 1971, the Department of External Affairs created the position of "post sinologist" to supplement its modest levels of expertise on China. Being fluent in Mandarin, I was appointed in 1991 to that role whose duties included reading all communications to and from the embassy, and alerting the Ambassador to anything warranting follow-up or attention.

In 1993 my embassy posting ended and I returned to Brock, but over the next five years I travelled frequently to China to help direct a massive collaboration between the Chinese Academy of Social Sciences (CASS) and the Royal Society of Canada (RSC).

―――

While the CCP is not given to taking outside advice on how to run a country, there are occasions when foreign experts are invited to help develop advice for reports that have at least the potential to inform China's policy-making process.

The CASS-RSC Democracy Project began in 1993 and ended in 1998. The Democracy Project was an ambitious attempt to promote gradual political reform by collaborating with an authoritarian administration inherently suspicious of external influences. The initiative was meant to help China explore the nature of democratic institutions in numerous nations. It seemed the Chinese officials involved wanted to know everything about how democracy functioned, ostensibly with a view to considering their own political reforms.

The project went to exhaustive lengths to explore the very essence of Canadian governance and political functions. China's delegates followed municipal election candidates canvassing door to door, were able to question historians and political scientists, and they met with political parties, speakers of provincial legislatures, NGO leaders and university presidents. They quizzed ombuds, judges, and lawyers to explore how legislative agendas are set, or who determines topics of debate in Parliament. They visited the Canadian Communist Party headquarters in Toronto.

Former heads of the CRTC and the Canada Council spoke about cultural policy, while prominent journalists like Knowlton Nash and Geoffrey Stevens discussed the role of news media. Specialists in tax policy, pensions and unemployment insurance explained how those structures work.

The Chinese asked interesting questions that often reflected the experiential chasms between two cultures, such as "After the quiet revolution in Quebec, what happened to the priests?" One day, passing a Zellers store with a prominent sign reading "The lowest price is the law," they wanted to know how this Canadian "lowest price law" is implemented and enforced.

After years of research, the Chinese group drafted extensive reports and recommendations for consideration by the CCP. The plan was for President Jiang Zemin — whose legacy was to have been democratic reform for China — to cap it off with a landmark speech in December 1998.

Alas, no such speech was ever given, and no democratizations launched. CCP leaders apparently felt they already had enough to deal with, managing public blowback at home over unpopular economic reforms, and they weren't about to start dangling the prospect of democracy in front of the people.

Through six years, the Democracy Project involved millions of dollars in travel, accommodation and organizational costs; scores of meetings with prominent Canadians and senior officials; and thousands of hours of logistical support from the federal civil service.

In the end, the only tangible impact seems to have been giving Beijing better ways to collect taxes. And even that acknowledgement only came to light when Premier Li Peng, speaking in 1996 with Prime Minister Jean Chrétien during a visit to China, briefly thanked Canada for providing advice on new taxation mechanisms.

Silently exiting the stage, the Democracy Project was finished.

In the 1990s Canada and the European Union had been using the United Nations as a platform to press China over human rights, including recurring reports of Tibetan, Uyghur and democracy groups being persecuted.

Irritated at being lectured on a global stage, Beijing tried changing the channel in 1997 by inviting Canada and the EU to a new series of "Bilateral Dialogues" where issues could be discussed, albeit in a carefully-controlled setting. These sessions succeeded in minimizing rebukes on the floor of the UN, but they generated no traction in advancing human rights.

In 2005 Canada's Ministry of Foreign Affairs asked me to conduct a review of these formal discussions and assess their effectiveness. I spent months interviewing scores of government officials in Ottawa and Beijing, NGOs, and officials from other participating governments.

The Dialogues were supposed to focus on how to implement the UN's human rights covenants, including judicial standards, policing, and prison conditions. But I quickly realized the process was a sham. Neither side was taking the talks seriously, and the outcomes did not change anyone's policy.

Western interviewees told me that China's cooperation declined steadily as its global power and influence increased. In Ottawa, incoming reports and updates rarely went any further than the Foreign Affairs administrative unit that was organizing Canada's participation. For their part, Chinese participants criticized Canadian presentations as being simplistic, shallow and lacking enough understanding of China's culture and politics to be useful.

My assessment, which spoke to the pervasive cynicism and "dialogue fatigue" among most officials, led to the Parliamentary Foreign Affairs Committee launching hearings to inform Canada's next steps. Once the report became public in 2006, other western governments agreed that the Dialogues were largely pointless.

In 2010, WikiLeaks released a trove of classified communiqués that senior U.S. officials had sent back to Washington, containing blunt talk about global issues. They included a 2007 cable to the State Department from Clark Randt, then U.S. Ambassador to China, in which he discussed my review of the Dialogues.

Randt wrote that U.S. diplomats had contacted human rights officers at numerous embassies in Beijing, and "Many pointed to a report . . .

completed by Canadian scholar Charles Burton as emblematic of their own experiences at the table with the Chinese."

"The report stated that the bilateral human rights dialogue process is indispensable as it allows a forum for western governments to voice their concerns about human rights violations in China. But worries persist that the substantive effect of the dialogues is insufficient."

"The report cites the following examples, among others:

> the Chinese take up much time in the formal meetings reading scripts;
>
> there is little connection between the dialogues and progress on human rights on the ground;
>
> China's (Ministry of Foreign Affairs) has downgraded the level of its head of delegation and has reduced staff in its Human Rights Division."

―――

In 2006, Jean-François Lesage — newly appointed China project officer for Canada's International Centre for Human Rights and Democratic Development — contacted me asking for advice on how to maximize his impact in the new job. (Rights and Democracy, as it was commonly called, was created by Parliament to promote values defined in the UN's Universal Declaration of Human Rights.)

Jean-François was in Beijing working on a contract for CIDA at the same time I was a diplomat at the embassy, though we didn't know each other. Now several years later he wanted to explore possible strategies to advance human rights in China.

I suggested he try and negotiate something with the Chinese Communist Party Central Committee School. Set in a magnificent but very high-security campus in Beijing, the School had two curriculum streams. One was for prospective or rising government officials, who studied political doctrine, party history, economics and other policy subjects.

The other channel was a more outward-looking research institute that helped develop graduate students.

In 2013 Xi Jinping would come to power and begin a new authoritarian era, where dissidents are imprisoned, ethnic groups "re-educated" and free expression squelched. Citizens dare not even write Xi's name in critical social media posts.

But during the 2000s China still enjoyed relative openness. It was in this climate that Jean-François made his pitch to the Central Party School. They quickly responded, and the new partners created an exchange program that included annual meetings alternating between Canada and China, involving researchers from the School.

Participants included people like Queen's University professor Will Kymlicka, the Canada Research Chair in Political Philosophy. I was struck that his work on multiculturalism was well known in the School; the Chinese delegates were very genuine in their interactions with him.

Our goal was to persuade CCP leadership to gradually integrate respect for human rights into their recurring rounds of policy formulation. But hopes of even incremental progress crashed under Xi Jinping, especially when compelling evidence led Canada, the Netherlands, the US and other nations to accuse China of committing genocide against its Uyghur population, and launching assimilationist policies toward Tibetans.

Thus another joint initiative to delicately advance human rights ended in futility.

In the midst of all of this, my close friend on the Party School delegation, Liu Jianhui, suffered a grievous tragedy when his daughter was brutally raped and murdered in her student room near York University in Toronto, all during a webcam call with a friend back in China.

When Liu and his wife came to Canada for the trial in 2014, I accompanied them to court daily. The heinous crime had stunned Canadians, and thousands of dollars were raised to help with their expenses.

One day when in their Toronto hotel room, I noticed the Sick Kids Hospital visible through the window and casually mentioned how grateful I was for the life-saving treatment my daughter had received there for a serious heart condition.

Months later, after the trial and the day before they returned to Beijing, the Lius donated to Sick Kids all of the money that had been raised for them.

With the trial concluded and the killer sentenced, Liu wrote a long letter of thanks to all the Canadians who had supported them during the ordeal. He asked me to translate it into English. The letter was published on the front page of the *Toronto Star*.

Being fluent in Mandarin (reading original PRC documents, watching PRC TV news in Chinese) helps provide insight into the strategies and intentions of the Chinese regime. An example is seen in this excerpt from a 2021 article I wrote for the Toronto Star, which references Xi Jinping's fiery scoffing at a statement that had been issued by the G7:

> *Xi himself made clear China "will not accept sanctimonious preaching from those who feel they have the right to lecture us," and such opponents of the PRC's policies of genocide and hostage diplomacy will "have their heads bashed bloody." The latter colourful phrase was edited out of the official English-language translation of the speech, but was enthusiastically cited in jingoist Chinese social media.*
>
> *There is an urgent need for Ottawa to fund programs that train young Canadians in contemporary Communist China studies, including Mandarin language studies.*

Chinese propagandists blatantly distort official statements through shameless mistranslation and subtle edits for foreign audiences.

In my early days of reading English versions of Communist Party materials, the translations were very poor. While the quality improved as China opened up to the West, some word choices put a different spin on meanings for the non-Chinese-reading audience. Today I notice much more willful distortion in translations coming out of Beijing, which is likely policy-directed as a subtle but effective form of disinformation.

Because of my background, I feel I can comprehend the nuanced implications of CCP texts better than Chinese people in Taiwan, Hong Kong or elsewhere outside the mainland. I think it is due to decades of closely following the CCP since the Cultural Revolution, then being immersed in conversation every waking hour with my Fudan University classmates during the years when China was transitioning from Mao's revolutionary model to the opening and reform of Deng.

Studying the History of Ancient Chinese Thought in Fudan's Department of Philosophy also honed my perceptive abilities. Like many multilingual people, my life of the mind in Chinese is highly distinctive from my life of the mind when I am thinking in English.

The modern era of Canada-China relations has been tortuous, fluctuating between cordial collaboration and diplomatic rage, commercial accord and vengeful trade boycotts, goodwill and icy polarization.

A precursor of the era of more strained relations was the 1989 Tiananmen Square massacre, when soldiers and tanks opened fire on or crushed unarmed pro-democracy student demonstrators. In the days that followed, Western governments — worried China was on the verge of chaos and instability — began evacuating their nationals.

Ottawa arranged flights to get most of its Embassy staff and all of their families out of China, as well as other Canadians who wanted to leave, mostly businesspeople or students. Many hunkered down in apartments or made their own way to the airport, but the Embassy also sent a van to several campuses to collect Canadian students.

Soldiers were maintaining rigid security around universities, and the van had to negotiate tense military lines. The students were eventually taken to the Embassy compound where they lived in tents for a few days before flying home. Getting them from the Embassy to the airport was similarly hairy.

Back home, meanwhile, Ottawa allowed Chinese nationals already in Canada to convert from student or visitor visas to permanent residency. Many or most did just that. This incensed Beijing, especially regarding those who had been sent to Canada on Chinese state funding.

The Canada-China relationship never fully got over that.

———

Xi Jinping's emergence as General Secretary of the Chinese Communist Party in 2013 was a signal moment in redefining the régime's place within its own narrative of Chinese history, and affirming what Beijing sees as an ancient mandate ordaining China as the supreme global power.

After becoming leader, Xi set about becoming dictator. He consolidated Party authority into one-man rule by removing term limits on his appointment and purging the very leadership group that had selected him in the first place. Having assumed the trifecta of Party General Secretary, Chairman of the Central Military Commission, and President "for life," Xi has made himself an emperor-like figure whose power exceeds all predecessors, including Chairman Mao.

This reframing of China's nationalism, and his control over it, is critical to Xi's ultimate thesis for global dominance: a Han master race presiding over the "Community of the Common Destiny of Mankind."

Xi contends that China will achieve universal prosperity by 2035 and will be the planet's undisputed power by 2050, thus rectifying perceived past humiliations of being subordinated by Japan and the west, and realizing Xi's vision of a China-led "community of the common destiny of mankind."

When the Xi regime looks at resource-rich Canada, it sees a remote region "under Heaven" rather than a sovereign nation with some inalienable right to control its own territory and domestic affairs.

For China, the message to Canadians is clear: America is the past and China is the future, so we must get on the right track. Canada had better realize the rewards are great for complying with China's political agenda, including its claim over Taiwan and military expansion in the East and South China Seas. Resistance is futile, and even the slightest opposition will have disastrous consequences for Canada's economy.

―――

In the 2020s, public opinion in the west toward China has been very negative, not just in Canada but in countries such as the US, Britain, Australia, Sweden, Germany and the Netherlands. By 2023 Canadian opinion reached an all-time low, fuelled by developments like Beijing's interference with ethnic communities in Canada, its attempts to manipulate Canada's elections, and of course the baseless detentions of innocent Canadians Michael Kovrig and Michael Spavor, and Kevin and Julia Garratt.

In the coming pages, a selection of previously published commentaries revisits some of those flashpoints as they were seen and/or experienced in the moment.

The media lens

YEARS OF BURTON ANALYSIS

SINCE CONFEDERATION, THE IMPORTANCE OF OPEN, honest commentary in the news media has helped Canadians collectively dissect, debate and better understand issues and choices that ultimately tell the world about our nation's priorities and moral compass.

In two decades of writing as a journalist (as opposed to as a diplomat, a professor, or an "official") I have been deeply gratified to have hundreds of opinion articles published in media outlets across Canada, literally from coast to coast.

For the first time, this book pulls a critical vein of those far-flung columns into a single collection. Whether or not people agree with my opinions, it is my dearest hope that this book gives readers a better grasp of how the incidents, the politics, the decisions and the motives have shaped the mercurial Canada-China relationship in the 21st century.

To help readers take their own path through the anthology, the years of articles are organized into distinct eras and themes. This is intended to let people prioritize their reading based on their own preferences.

They are as follows:

- The era of Prime Minister Stephen Harper
- The era of Prime Minister Justin Trudeau
- Hostage Diplomacy
- Huawei and Canada's 5G security
- The Coronavirus
- Canada's sovereignty vs China and Trump

THE STEPHEN HARPER ERA

Just as Prime Minister Jean Chrétien's "quiet diplomacy" in the 1990s failed to persuade China to become a responsible global stakeholder and uphold its own citizens' human rights, Prime Minister Stephen Harper likewise could not overcome the gulf between Canada's liberal-democratic institutions and Beijing's rigidly managed relations with the West.

A more sophisticated engagement with China

THE GLOBE AND MAIL, 30 NOVEMBER 2009

ALL THE FEDERAL POLITICAL PARTIES AGREE that Canada's priorities with regard to China are, first, to promote our prosperity through trade and investment between the countries and, second, to encourage high-quality Chinese immigrants to move here.

We also want to collaborate with China in areas of concern such as fair trade, environmental sustainability, the spread of communicable diseases, respect for human rights, transnational crime and dozens of other issues that arise in a rapidly globalizing world. There is little room for partisan disagreement on any of this.

Moreover, people of all political stripes are concerned by reports of human-rights abuses in China. Canadians stand for freedom of expression, the right to religious and political freedom and the right to private property free from expropriation through corrupt deals. Even a "sensitive" political initiative such as extending honorary Canadian citizenship to the Dalai Lama was passed unanimously in the House of Commons.

Internationally, Beijing's support for repressive and dangerous regimes in Myanmar, Sudan, North Korea, Zimbabwe and other places is worrying, and Canada would like to persuade China of the benefits of becoming a more responsible citizen in the international community.

So whoever forms the next government in Ottawa will probably continue to respect Canada's fundamental interests in its relations with China. The main factor distinguishing the Liberals from the Conservatives, NDP and Bloc Québécois is in the area of human rights.

Liberals support the "quiet diplomacy" adopted by Jean Chrétien, who initiated a government-to-government secret dialogue on human rights in 1997. Beijing's standard response to Canadian concerns about human-rights abuses is that China hopes to eventually become democratic with an impartial and independent judiciary, but developmental and cultural factors make this impossible for the time being.

This line of argument wears thinner as the years go by and reports continue unabated of arbitrary arrest, torture and repression, including pervasive Internet censorship.

In 2006, the Conservatives suspended this dialogue because it was seen as ineffective in furthering human rights in China. An important consideration is the concern that Ottawa's approach may correlate to our realization of Canadian economic interests in China. If Canada is vocal on human rights, does this have a negative impact on our ability to sell Canadian products in China?

It is fair to conclude that "quiet diplomacy" with China has not benefited Canada economically. Over the decade since Ottawa began its annual secret dialogue with Beijing as the primary mode of engaging

China over human-rights violations, the country's share of Chinese imports dropped by a third.

Our trade imbalance with China should be a major cause for concern. According to Industry Canada statistics, Canadian merchandise exports to China in 2008 amounted to $10.1-billion, but imports were valued at $42.6-billion. That's a huge trade deficit, about 4 to 1.

In sharp contrast, Australia had a ratio of 1.53 to 1 this year, thanks to 45-per-cent growth in its exports to China over the past year compared with only 19.5-per-cent growth in imports.

Moreover, according to a report in *The Globe and Mail* last month, 130,000 Chinese are studying in Australia, compared with 42,000 in Canada.

As Prime Minister Stephen Harper prepares to visit Beijing this week, we need a major reboot of the way Canada engages China. Most of the younger Chinese diplomats in Canada have near-fluency in English, and many have graduate degrees from universities in Canada, the United States, Australia or Britain. We need to be sending comparably qualified Canadians to China, preferably people who have done advanced study there. But we are not doing that.

We need to do a major government-led overhaul of how Canada does its trade promotion in China. We need much more sophisticated engagement in the Chinese political system in general.

Canada needs a clear strategy for better access to the Chinese market, one that factors in the distinct characteristics of Chinese culture and Canada's comparative advantage in that market vis-à-vis our competitors. China requires comprehensive engagement, and our approach must extend beyond conventional diplomatic channels.

For example, Ottawa should engage Chinese policy-makers in both the government and in the Communist Party, all of whose decisions have implications for our interests. The focus on China's Ministry of Foreign Affairs and International Co-operation should be expanded to a more comprehensive engagement of the Chinese system. Canadian diplomats need to better recognize that many of the most influential players in the Chinese system are in Communist Party institutions.

Hopefully, with the Conservative government less preoccupied by the prospect of a general election than it has been in the past three years, more focus can be placed on foreign policy and the importance of Canada's being more effective in realizing its interests in China and elsewhere.

Bon voyage, Mr. Harper.

When the G20 was created in 1999, China was included in this forum for finance ministers and central bankers from 20 of the world's largest established and emerging economies. However Beijing's tendency to strong-arm trading partners into positions of disadvantage, and also to support Third World dictators, led the original G8 group of nations to reconstitute its smaller group, with China excluded. (The larger G20 still exists, with China as a member.) But the challenge was clear: how to integrate China into a world order based on principles of fairness, transparency, honesty and respect for universal norms of human rights.

Economic titan China needs to act like a leader

TORONTO STAR, 17 JUNE 2010

NEXT WEEK, CANADA WILL HOST MEETINGS that will see the G20 displace the G8 as the leading forum of industrialized nations. The meetings (G8 in Huntsville on June 25–26, and G20 in Toronto on June 26–27) will be a formal acknowledgement by the international community of the important new reality of China's rise to global power.

After 35 years as the main institution for coordinating international economic order, the G8 — which does not include China — will be overtaken by a newly assertive G20. And many see the G20 as centred on a G2, China and the United States.

Without question, a central challenge of our times is how to fully integrate China into an international order based on principles of reciprocal fairness, transparency, honesty and respect for universal norms of human rights.

There are several aspects of China's international policies that fall short of these principles. First of all, China does not allow fair access to its market as it should under the terms of China's accession to the World Trade Organization in 2001. Canada has a 4:1 trade deficit with China and the gap is widening year by year. A central factor in this is China's refusal to value its currency at a fair market exchange rate. Due to Chinese government-mandated currency rates determined by a secret process, Canadian products and services are less competitive in the Chinese market.

Related to this is the pervasive lack of protection for the intellectual property rights of Canadian manufacturers in China. This is buttressed by aggressive industrial espionage programs run out of Chinese embassies and consulates in Canada and throughout the world. Moreover, Canadian firms in China have difficulty enforcing contracts there due to China's lack of an independent judiciary. Canada has been trying since 1994 to negotiate a Foreign Investment Protection Agreement with Beijing, but there is little in it for China as its firms and investors are already well protected by the rule of law here in Canada. So Canada loses again.

The truth is that China would do better to comply with accepted mutually beneficial international norms of trade and investment. Engaging in trade based on principles of reciprocal fairness, transparency and honesty would benefit China in the long run. China's imposition of so many non-tariff barriers to access its market is simply not good economics, not by any measure.

Another area of concern about China's leading role in the G20 is Beijing's well-documented support for dictators and tyrants in exchange for short-term economic benefits. China plays a role in propping up most of the world's autocratic regimes.

In the case of regimes that most seriously threaten world peace — such as Iran, Sudan and North Korea — China offers economic aid and manipulates its veto power in the UN Security Council to shield serious human rights violators or nuclear weapon proliferators from UN sanctions. In return, China derives privileged access to natural resources under the regimes' control, especially oil and gas, and in ways that not only do not benefit local inhabitants but often poison the environment, affecting farming, fishing and the health of residents.

In addition to bribes and corrupt payments funnelled to the elites of brutal dictatorships, Beijing supports these regimes through donations of prestige projects such as public squares, sports stadiums and extravagant presidential palaces — often in lands where much of the population is struggling to fend off famine and ethnic repression.

China has no qualms about feeding the deluded egos of tyrants who yearn for respect. The Chinese Foreign Affairs University even extended an honorary doctorate to Robert Mugabe, noting his "brilliant contribution" to diplomacy and international relations and characterizing him as "a man of strong convictions, a man of great achievements, a man devoted to preserving world peace." It is humiliating for the citizens of China to be associated with such diplomatic absurdity.

Likewise, North Korea receives huge quantities of food aid from China, along with oil inputs to keep its economy from utter collapse, and 80 per cent of its consumer goods. Beijing is also instrumental in deferring international action against North Korea by hypocritically manipulating the Six-Party Talks process. Meanwhile, North Korea remains a menace to the peaceful interests of the global community by offering weaponry and nuclear technology to very unsavoury customers.

There are now indications that North Korea is providing Burma the ability to build a nuclear device. This is a real cause for concern, but China could readily play a more assertive role in Burma and facilitate the assumption of power by Aung San Suu Kyi. A stable, democratic Burma on China's border would be a much more sound neighbour and strategic trading partner than the irrational and unpredictable military regime crumbling there now.

In North Korea, only China has the capacity to assist in a stable political transition by engaging progressive military elements over whom Beijing has influence. Again, the trade and investment possibilities for China in reconstructing the devastated North, once the irrational and unpredictable Kim family regime is replaced, would be enormous.

China's prominent role in the G20 can undoubtedly be a good thing, but the expectation must be that it exhibit values of statesmanship and global leadership and act on them in very short order — in its own interest and in the interests of a peaceful, prosperous and just world.

Encouraging this process should be a priority for all the G20 member nations.

China's most wanted fugitive Lai Changxing was deported from Canada to China to face charges of running billion-dollar smuggling rings. The extradition followed a thorough Canadian review that was insulated from political interference, but people in China weren't buying that part. They were certain that pressure on Canadian officials is what got the result, just as it would in China. After a show trial where Beijing's "evidence" did not meet international legal standards, Lai was sentenced to life in prison. China's earlier promises that Canadian officials would get access to Lai in prison were never fulfilled.

Farewell, Mr. Lai

THE GLOBE AND MAIL, 25 JULY 2011

ON THURSDAY, BARELY 24 HOURS AFTER Foreign Affairs Minister John Baird ended his fence-mending visit to Beijing and Shanghai, a Canadian judge refused to stay the deportation order of China's most wanted fugitive, calling him a "common criminal."

Lai Changxing, accused of masterminding a multibillion-dollar smuggling operation that imported consumer goods without paying custom duties, has been a major topic of conversation among my friends and neighbours here in Kunming, in southwestern China. They put a highly political spin on it, seeing the Federal Court's rejection of his refugee claim as a significant gesture on the part of the Harper government to demonstrate goodwill to Beijing. My emphatic assertions that Canada's judiciary is not amenable to political pressure from the government and that the timing of Mr. Baird's trip was just a coincidence are flatly dismissed with knowing Chinese smiles.

Nevertheless, I was somewhat relieved to hear of the decision to send back Mr. Lai. If, as soon as Mr. Baird left the country, it emerged that Mr. Lai would never face trial in China, outrage against Canada would have been marked, to say the least. Allegations that Mr. Lai had been supporting himself in Canada with an illegal gambling operation and reports of extensive associations with loan sharking and a Chinese triad called the Big Circle Boys have been extensively detailed in the Chinese media.

I first learned about Lai Changxing in 1999, when I was a political officer at the Canadian embassy in Beijing. Chinese authorities informed us that corrupt police had tipped off Mr. Lai that he was about to be arrested on charges of smuggling, tax evasion and bribery. Using fraudulently obtained Hong Kong documents, he entered Canada as a tourist. So the Chinese government asked the embassy to arrange for Mr. Lai to be repatriated back to China right away, on the next plane home if possible. Oh, that it could have been so easy!

The Lai case cast a shadow over Canada-China relations for the next several years. Beijing authorities seemed convinced that, if they exerted enough pressure on their friends in Jean Chrétien's government, then Mr. Lai would be sent back without further ado. Unsubstantiated rumours that Mr. Lai was withholding evidence that he had bribed close associates of senior Communist leaders evidently intensified the desire of Chinese ambassadors and government officials for Mr. Lai's return, so much so that, sometimes, there were menacing diplomatic undertones of "or else." Clearly, Ottawa was under a lot of pressure from Beijing.

In 2001, I was asked to serve as a witness for the Canadian government's side at Mr. Lai's refugee hearing. In preparation, I was sent boxes containing thousands of pages of Chinese government documents detailing their case against Mr. Lai. Much of the criminal schemes, according to the documents, seemed brilliantly simple: Bring a shipping container of tax-free cigarettes into the port of Xiamen. Break the seal on the container, remove contraband cigarettes, replace with rope. Bribe the customs to reseal the container. Pay minuscule duty on the "rope imports." Repeat the next day with the same rope.

Mr. Lai's application for Canadian refugee status was eventually rejected, but it was hard not to be impressed by the process. Arguments made by Mr. Lai's lawyer, David Matas, and the ruling by members of the International Refugee Board and later by Mr. Justice Yves de Montigny of the Federal Court showed a degree of erudition that was humbling to me.

Over subsequent years, Mr. Lai's legal team mounted a series of appeals and delaying motions. The Canadian government spent millions to match the similar amounts Mr. Lai was paying for his defence. To my knowledge, none of his lawyers worked for free, and the money he was paying them may have come from the proceeds of crime. The fact that Mr. Lai may have used allegedly "dirty money" to stave off his repatriation to China is highly troubling.

I do worry about what fate will meet Mr. Lai in China. Will he be tortured in the course of interrogation? Could he die under murky circumstances in prison, as his brother and his accountant already have?

But I also have complete faith in the legal judgment of Mr. Justice Michel Shore, who approved Mr. Lai's deportation. Whatever my friends and neighbours in Kunming may think, I'm convinced that Canada's justice system is second to none and that Mr. Lai has received his due process of Canadian law. As someone who has spent a lot of my life living as an expatriate under an authoritarian regime, I very much appreciate that Canada's independent and incorruptible judiciary is one of the things that makes Canada a truly great country.

Returning Mr. Lai to China sends a clear signal: Canada is not a country where international criminals can seek refuge. But the facts of Mr. Lai's case are troubling all the same.

The trade deficit with China was getting worse, Canada imported four times more than it exported. By 2012 Canadian ministers were accelerating visits to China, promoting an accord that boosted trade while protecting investors from China's unfair practices. But such talks had been going nowhere for 20 years. Businesses were nervous dealing with a country where foreign investors faced difficulty getting compensation for their losses in cases where promised protection of proprietary processes were not fulfilled. Chinese investors in Canada face no such risks.

Harper in China: Juggling oil sales and core principles

TORONTO STAR, 4 FEBRUARY 2012

THE ECONOMIC EMPHASIS OF PRIME MINISTER Stephen Harper's second trip to China is ultimately linked to Canada-U.S. relations. China is the new engine of global prosperity, and here at home concern is growing that our reliance on the battered U.S. economy will precipitate a long economic decline in Canada.

Indeed, John Baird made a statement about Ottawa's changing agenda last summer by choosing China for his first official visit as foreign affairs minister, only travelling to Washington some weeks later.

Ed Fast, new minister of international trade, likewise made an official visit to China this fall prior to his first official visit to Washington.

Canada does not do well in the booming Chinese market. The trade imbalance is 4 to 1 in China's favour, and over the past decade our exports have actually lost market share as the U.S., Europe and Australia implemented more China-proactive policies. Consequently, Fast has increasingly been voicing his support for, at long last, establishing a Canada-China Foreign Investment Promotion and Protection Agreement (FIPA).

One reason for Canada's weak showing is that Canadian investors are nervous about doing business in a country that rejects separation of powers between the judicial, legislative and executive branches of government. Unlike most of our trading partners, China's judiciary is not independent, falling under the leadership of the Chinese Communist Party. Local courts cannot rule impartially if directed otherwise by high-level authorities. So in cases of breach of contract, Canadian investors in China have difficulty getting compensation for their losses, especially in cases where promised protections of proprietary industrial processes have not been maintained.

But negotiations on this FIPA have been dragging on since 1994, with more than a dozen rounds of talks since 2004 alone. And it is very unlikely that Harper will be signing any trade accords on this trip.

Why? There is little incentive for China to negotiate such an agreement. Chinese investment in Canada is already protected by our rule of law and our transparent and fair business regulations. Terms like "reciprocal fairness" or "level playing field" are not in the Chinese leadership's vocabulary, and Canada can like it or lump it.

The failed FIPA negotiations mirror 15 years of failed western dialogue with China over human rights. If anything, human rights have actually deteriorated since the dialogues began in 1997. The Communist Party recently proposed a law allowing detention for up to six months, in undisclosed locations, without charge or trial. This is already happening to human rights lawyers and political activists. Some who are eventually released tell harrowing tales of physical and psychological torture. Others have simply disappeared, and prospects of their return appear bleak.

For this trip, there is no indication Prime Minister Harper will take a softer line on China's human rights record than he has in the past. Just last month, for instance, Foreign Minister Baird renewed Ottawa's criticism of China's crackdown on religious freedom.

Beijing might to respond to Harper's human rights engagement with the usual plea for understanding: China will respect human rights eventually, however its low state of development, and the legacy of its culture and history, do not allow for implementation of human rights measures just now.

But judging by recent remarks from President Hu Jintao, raising human rights this time around will more likely get Harper a sharp rebuke. Then the talk will move on to trade, and this is when Beijing will quickly buy any oil that Canada can't pipe south to the U.S.

It won't be a hard sell for us, because China much prefers to depend on energy supplies from a politically stable liberal democracy like Canada. Beijing's support for Col. Gadhafi ended up costing China millions in lost infrastructure investment after rebels toppled the Libyan dictator. And China's other oil-rich friends, like Iran and Sudan, are similarly vulnerable to potential disruptions depending on the vagaries of domestic politics and the international environment.

Selling our oil to China via the controversial Northern Gateway pipeline would do much to redress Canada's trade shortfall, and during the Prime Minister's visit we will no doubt hear expressions of enthusiasm by Chinese state-owned firms anxious to invest in Canadian energy projects.

Herein lies the rub.

The heads of these companies are mostly appointed by the Chinese Communist Party. For them, enterprise management is not just doing business, it is a personal career path to senior government and party posts. They answer to the party, not to their companies' boards of directors.

In wanting more latitude to invest in Canada, China's state-owned enterprises will also want to seek capital in Canadian markets and list on Canadian stock exchanges. But some of these companies bring practices from a "wild west" business culture that fall far short of standards required of companies listing on Canadian exchanges. Think falsifying accounts to overstate revenues and understate obligations; fabricating claimed contracts; tax evasion; off-the-books diversion of large sums to the personal accounts of executives; and using bribes or kickbacks to gain advantage in contract bids.

The research firm Muddy Waters, which monitors business practices in China, recently reported that fiscal malfeasance by Chinese businesses listed on foreign exchanges are likely just the tip of a large iceberg. Chinese companies operating abroad often disregard intellectual property rights and proprietary production processes, and recruit economic spies to engage in cyber-espionage and steal commercial or government secrets in order to further the interests of the Chinese state.

The Harper trip is all about increasing trade activity between Canada and China, which Canada needs if our economy is to continue to grow and create jobs in the years and decades ahead. But Canada's national interests will be best served by a prudent, principled and informed approach to China.

China would never allow foreign ownership of energy or resource sectors considered crucial to national security, yet Stephen Harper approves the $15.1-billion sale of Canadian energy giant Nexen to a Chinese state-owned oil company. Harper's decision follows months of national debate, lobbying from Beijing, and public opposition in Canada. He said it would be the last sale of Canada's resource sector to a foreign government-owned enterprise, but since then China's bids to buy and control minerals critical for defence and green technologies have been met with political ambiguity.

Stephen Harper's new trade rules safeguard Canada's interests

THE GLOBE AND MAIL, 8 DECEMBER 2012

"When we say that Canada is open for business, we do not mean that Canada is for sale to foreign governments." — Prime Minister Stephen Harper, Dec. 7, 2012

LATE ON FRIDAY AFTERNOON, AFTER THE markets had closed, Prime Minister Stephen Harper announced the federal government will allow the Chinese National Off-Shore Oil Corporation to purchase Canada's Nexen, thereby converting Nexen into a Chinese state-owned enterprise. In the same breath, however, he also said there will be no further Chinese state acquisitions relating to Canada's oilsands.

Was the PM looking out for Canadian interests?

After months of debate in the media, and strong opposition from most Canadians, the decision to approve the Chinese state purchase of a Canadian company this one last time should mitigate against angry diplomatic retaliation by Beijing. But in reality it is hard for Beijing to protest a decision limiting China's future investments in Canada when China would never allow foreign acquisition of its own major firms, especially in the energy and resource sectors that China defines as critical to its national security.

Moreover, the "Statement Regarding Investment by Foreign State-Owned Enterprises," issued by Industry Canada minutes before Mr. Harper's announcement, goes a lot further in promulgating rules to protect Canada's economic sovereignty. For instance, it indicates that in applying the Investment Canada Act, the federal Minister of Industry will carefully monitor state-owned enterprise transactions throughout the Canadian economy to determine if they are of net benefit to Canada.

It also says the minister will scrutinize how much control or influence any state-owned enterprise might exert on Canadian businesses being acquired; how much the state-owned enterprise might influence the industry in which the Canadian business operates; and how much a foreign government might control the state-owned enterprise acquiring the Canadian business.

In other words, whenever acquisitions by state-owned enterprises could undermine the private-sector orientation of an industrial sector — and subject it to foreign state influence — Ottawa will act to safeguard Canadian interests.

The bottom line is clear. If China were to follow up its Nexen acquisition with other large investments and become a significant player in Canada's economy, the consequences go far beyond simply which nation would benefit economically from Canada's resources.

It would also give China considerable leverage over Canada's policies on the environment, or labour standards. And the Chinese Party-state would naturally demand that Canada stop voicing concerns about issues that matter to most Canadians, including China's repressive policies in Tibet and Xinjiang; Chinese state harassment of Tibetans, Uyghurs and supporters of Chinese human rights and democracy in Canada; Chinese espionage, including computer hacking leading to theft of Canadian intellectual property and strategic technologies; and China's support for rogue regimes — such a s North Korea, Iran, Sudan, Zimbabwe or Venezuela — that threaten world peace.

In 2006, Mr. Harper said, "I think Canadians want us to promote our trade relations worldwide — and we do that — but I don't think Canadians want us to sell out important Canadian values. They don't want us to sell that out to the almighty dollar."

Six years later, in an increasingly complex diplomatic environment, it seems his position still holds true.

Kevin and Julia Garrett had been languishing in Chinese jail cells for three months when Prime Minister Stephen Harper decided at the last minute to attend an Asia-Pacific Economic Conference hosted by Beijing. This article examines factors behind his about-face: trade deals for Canadian businesses, appealing to ethnic Chinese voters in Canada — and not wanting to appear disrespectful to the regime in Beijing.

Why did Harper go to China? The ethnic vote. And money

THE GLOBE AND MAIL, 10 NOVEMBER 2014

PRIME MINISTER STEPHEN HARPER CERTAINLY HAD valid excuses for initially deciding to skip the Asia Pacific Economic Cooperation Summit in China, and cancel his pre-summit official visit to China.

For one, APEC conflicted with Remembrance Day ceremonies at home, just weeks after the murder of two Canadian soldiers on home soil. Not going to China also made sense in light of Beijing's lack of response to Ottawa's concerns over significant issues in the Canada-China relationship. As well, Canada has not had an official visit from the president of China since 2010; it's their turn to come to us. And anyway, the Prime Minister will see most of the same world leaders at this weekend's G20 in Australia. He could just as well sit down with the President of China and try to sort things out then.

But at the 11th hour, the Prime Minister's Office announced he would travel to China after all. As Mr. Harper put it, the Chinese government "really wanted me to be here" for the opening of the APEC summit.

Of course, not insignificant factors of money and ethnic voters also contributed to this change of heart. Lobby groups — representing Canadian businesses with relationships with Chinese communist state firms, as well as associations largely composed of recent immigrants from the PRC — predicted dire consequences for Canadian interests in China if our PM showed "disrespect" by not attending APEC in Beijing. They compared it to the offense Mr. Harper purportedly caused when he decided not to attend the Beijing Olympics in 2008.

(Not that this goes both ways. In 2012 the Chinese delegation to the London Olympics was led not by the President or even the second-ranked Premier of the State Council, but by one Liu Qi, "deputy-director of the Central Commission for Guiding Ethic and Cultural Progress". Doubtless no offence to the host U.K. was intended, and likely none taken.)

Chinese media reports of the Harper visit focused on boosting relations, increasing trade and "building mutual trust." This seems to mean trusting Beijing's assurances that Ottawa should have no cause for concern about allegations of pervasive human rights abuse in China, or about Chinese cyber espionage threatening Canadian security. Indeed there were many photographs of Mr. Harper and his accompanying cabinet ministers laughing and smiling and giving the impression that they thoroughly enjoyed interacting with leaders of the Chinese Communist Party.

But it is hard to imagine that Mr. Harper was genuinely building bonds of friendship at his lengthy Friday meeting with Xiao Baolong, the Communist Party Secretary of Zhejiang province. Mr. Xiao is currently currying favour with the leadership in Beijing by systematically suppressing Christianity. Hundreds of churches have been ordered to remove visible crosses from their buildings, and many churches have been completely razed on the premise of "building code violations" — including the heart-rending destruction of the magnificent, recently constructed 3,000-seat Sanjiang Cathedral.

At another event, the Prime Minister felt compelled to hold his tongue at a press conference when Chinese Premier Li Keqiang responded to a question about the incarceration and intensive interrogation of Canadians Kevin and Julia Garratt, who have been held separately in isolation for more than three months without charge. Mr. Li suggested China is "a country under the rule of law, and there is clear stipulation in Chinese constitutional law that human rights must be respected and protected."

So did Mr. Harper and his delegation spend 26 hours on a plane to China and back, only to be subjected to this sort of absurd blather?

For Canada, the much-trumpeted take-away — the reward for paying tribute to the Chinese regime — was a ceremony where, in Mr. Harper's presence, 18 contracts and memoranda of understanding were signed, purportedly worth $2.5-billion in business and trade. That these are mostly pre-existing agreements or are early agreements to negotiate deals, many of which never come to fruition, is not as important as the symbolic value. And Ottawa seems overly delighted that Beijing will now let us trade with them in Canadian currency, rather than the past practice of U.S. dollars only.

The real bottom line is that the Chinese leadership got the affirmation of political legitimacy that they wanted from Canada. There would have been troubling questions by people in China if the group photos of APEC leaders lacked Mr. Harper because he decided that Canada would be better off if he just stayed home.

In Beijing, Mr. Harper did affirm that Canadian interests in China consist in all three aspects of promoting Canadian prosperity, ensuring Canadian security and standing true to Canadian values in our interactions with the PRC. But in the end, as Mr. Harper tentatively expressed it, "I think we have significantly advanced the economic relationship." Time will tell if he is right on this.

After John Baird stunned Parliament by abruptly resigning as Foreign Affairs Minister and as an MP, this column considered his legacy. As Canada's senior player in international relations, Baird was prone to bootlicking when dealing with China, letting Canada's relationship become one of subservience while patronizing Beijing with platitudes that ignored its shameful human rights record. He did not even press China to resolve the case of jailed Canadian missionaries Kevin and Julia Garratt.

Bending over backward for Beijing

NATIONAL POST, 5 MARCH 2015

ROB NICHOLSON HAS HIS WORK CUT out. A month after John Baird abruptly quit as Canada's ineffectual foreign affairs minister, his successor is watching for starting points to strengthen Canada's hand in its relationship with the world's most important economy.

Whatever his value to the Prime Minister as a parliamentary pit bull, Mr. Baird's legacy as foreign minister is one of failure and bombast. His jagged and often unprovoked political rhetoric on Israel and the Middle East negatively changed how people around the world view Canada and its values. In Egypt, Canadian journalist Mohamed Fahmy, still hoping to be deported home from his nightmare, blames Mr. Baird's ham-fisted verbosity for sabotaging the Canadian citizen's prospects of freedom.

But it is on the China file where Canada has suffered the most. During Mr. Baird's time as foreign minister, Canada showed undue weakness in dealings with Beijing.

It did not start out looking that way. In 2011, when the PM gave Mr. Baird the Foreign Affairs portfolio, it was seen as evidence of the government's stated desire for "principled foreign policy." And when Mr. Baird selected China for his first official visit, it seemed the Tories were getting serious about pursuing Canada's interests in the Asia-Pacific.

Disappointments, however, came quickly. On that first trip, Mr. Baird did not publicly mention human rights, or reiterate Canada's condemnation of China's support of brutal Third World regimes. If anything he appeased his hosts by referring to China as a "friend" and "important ally," categorizing China's repressive non-democratic state in the same terms as nations that share our values and political perspectives, such as Britain, France and the United States.

As for "principled foreign policy," the government of new Chinese leader Xi Jinping is the most repressive since the end of the horrendous Cultural Revolution 35 years ago. Besides enhanced censorship of news media and the Internet, and a campaign to suppress "Western influences," new measures have been implemented to make foreign businesses less competitive in China.

China is also conducting a purge of those who oppose Mr. Xi's leadership in the military, security apparatus and senior elements associated with his predecessor, Hu Jintao. The secret process purportedly investigating "corruption" is simply a tactic to remove political challengers. It's true that Communist officials seldom have lifestyles that reflect their modest official salaries, but this includes Mr. Xi himself. His annual pay is $22,256, yet he somehow manages to send his daughter to Harvard (and is clearly untroubled by the threat of "Western influences" on her).

And now this anti-graft campaign reaches into Canada — with Ottawa's blessing. Remarkably, Canada has agreed to a pact with China to cover "the return of property related to people who would have fled to Canada and would have been involved in corrupt activities," as Canada's ambassador to China, Guy Saint-Jacques, said in an interview with the *China Daily*. Unfortunately we will have to take Beijing's word on whose bank deposits and houses and businesses we will be handing over, because under the pact Canada has no guarantee of due process of law. Such assurances do not exist in a Chinese system that has no independent, impartial judiciary.

That pact was followed by the treaty Canada signed last year, also on Mr. Baird's watch, to exchange information on Customs investigations. This agreement seems particularly wrong-headed for us, since China's state enterprises are evidently behind much illegal export of Canadian classified and proprietary technology in the military and commercial sectors. Why would we give China a heads-up on our interdiction methods, all the better for them to figure out how to evade them?

In both of these deals, Canada caved in to Chinese demands with no assurance of reciprocal concessions, or Beijing even acknowledging our concerns about market access and human rights. Case in point: Before announcing the above two agreements, we did not even press China to resolve the case of Canadians Kevin and Julia Garratt, missionaries arrested last year on ill-explained charges and who continue to be held in China.

John Baird was not strong or principled enough in shaping Canada's relations with Beijing. Severe restrictions on Canadian involvement in China's economy were not resolved by the recent Canada-China Foreign Investment Protection Agreement; Chinese cyber, economic and military espionage remains a very serious threat to Canada's security; and China's human rights violations have become worse, not better, under Xi Jinping. Even the 2010 Nobel Peace Prize Laureate, Liu Xiaobo, remains incommunicado in prison.

Mr. Baird's time as foreign minister left economic relations stacked against Canada, but at least his departure is giving Mr. Harper an opening to re-think how best to realize Canadian interests in an emerging China.

For the 2015 Chinese National People's Congress, this column takes readers into the Great Hall of the People to get a sense of not just economic and policy talk, but of China's entrenched culture and the complexities that poses for CCP leadership. Burton picks up on the national dialogues and provides ground-level glimpses of a communist superpower staging its annual pantomime of democracy.

More than empty rhetoric as China engages in Communist democracy

THE GLOBE AND MAIL, 6 MARCH 2015

WHEN THE CHINESE NATIONAL PEOPLE'S CONGRESS opens an annual meeting, as it did this week in Beijing, any resemblance to a democratic legislature is purely accidental.

It only meets for 10 days a year, its members are not elected, do not represent any constituency or opposition party, and most have full-time jobs in government and business (though there is a scattering of Buddhist monks and ethnic minorities in colourful national dress among them, to give a veneer of inclusiveness). There's also very little actual debating, though a lot of votes will take place over the 10 days, and it's safe to expect a "yes" vote of well over 90 per cent on each measure the government introduces.

The first order of business was the Work Report, where Premier Li Keqiang rhymed off government accomplishments from the past year, including preventing Ebola from spreading into China, good news about significant reduction in industrial accidents, and measures to improve food safety. (Food safety is a major concern of Chinese consumers, for good reason). The recounting of government successes goes on and on, and the 2,964 delegates in the Great Hall of the People were under strict instructions not to check social media or play games on cellphones while the Premier was reading his report. Last year this was a bit of a problem.

When the review ended and the Premier turned to plans for the year ahead, there were alarm bells in his words, in terms of China's economy and its effect on domestic social stability.

The main concern is that the government is predicting "only" 7 per cent growth in the next year — the "new normal" as Mr. Li termed it. This sounds like a lot of economic expansion compared to growth rates in developed nations (Canada would be delighted with half that rate), but it is a considerable slowdown from the double-digit growth China has experienced over the last 30 years.

Mr. Li said overcapacity is a big problem, maintaining stable growth has become difficult, and "growth in investment is sluggish." In fact, the biggest burden on China's economy is its dominance by state-owned enterprises that are inefficient due to corruption, political demands on them and the lack of incentive for innovation.

This adds up to a potential big danger for a nation with a largely undeveloped social safety net. When Mr. Li warned that "in times of peace we must be alert to danger; in times of stability we must be mindful of the potential for chaos," it was not empty rhetoric.

How China plans to respond to this threat appears more aspirational than realistic. Mr. Li spoke of improving government administrative capacity to enhance "public credibility," and said officials should avoid "capriciousness" and "hedonism and extravagance," but he was hazy on exactly how to change this deeply entrenched culture. In the past year alone, 39 members of the National People's Congress have been expelled for corruption. China's own statistics put the combined net worth of delegates to the National People's Congress and the Chinese People's Political Consultative Conference at $576.4-billion — more than the total GDP of a country like Austria. And more than 200 of the delegates meeting this week are billionaires in their own right. Evidently the Chinese Communist Party has been very good to them.

In the face of this, he did announce (again, without details) there will be new measures to address pollution, expanded public services including medical and elder care, and provision of education for rural children. And, he said, the government will "keep the economy resilient despite downward pressure on it" and "continue the struggle against corruption."

But as the chasm between China's rich and poor widens each year, Mr. Li recognizes the dangerous cleavage between those who don't have enough and are disgruntled about it, and those who have crazy wealth and flaunt it with extreme luxury consumption, wearing expensive jewelry as they drive around China's cities in Ferraris and Lamborghinis.

This alienation by corruptly obtained wealth of the political and business elite, from the workers and farmers that the Party once purported to represent, is the nub of a growing crisis. It all constitutes the potential lurking danger and chaos that Mr. Li alluded to, if things don't go as the Work Report promises.

As for the global audience, the opening day of Congress was likewise less than encouraging. Mr. Li said Chinese missions abroad will become more proactive asserting the interests of China's state-owned enterprises abroad, as part and parcel of the government's economic agenda, and Beijing will also work to "strengthen the bonds of attachment with Chinese living abroad." This does not bode well for the coming year of Canada-China relations.

Having spent extended periods of time in China, living closely among classmates or neighbours in their daily routines, helps Burton sense and reflect the national character, including how people are wary of what their government tells them — just like other people around the world. This familiarity is invaluable as he gives non-Chinese readers an authentic grassroots take of China's domestic economic roiling.

Taking stock of the Chinese stock market slide

THE GLOBE AND MAIL, 8 JULY 2015

THE PAST YEAR WAS A HOT one for investors in China's stock market, as the index shot up 150 per cent over 12 months. But in a long overdue correction, Chinese stocks have lost, on average, 30 per cent of their value since the middle of June.

The government-controlled press offers assurances that China's economic fundamentals are sound, but government efforts to support stock prices, relax margin rules and cut benchmark interest rates appear to be having little positive effect. Most Chinese don't believe the government's statements, and the more the government tries to instill investor confidence, the more people suspect that things are even worse than they're being told.

With 90 million investors, China's daily stock market turnover is bigger than that of the United States. About 80 per cent of investors tend to be small retail investors, people whose risky stock portfolio is both their medical insurance plan and retirement savings.

The Chinese market's problems begin at a fundamental level. In general, the numbers reported by Chinese state firms and enterprises lack credibility, and few people have access to any knowledge that could make them better-informed investors. Financial investigators or reporters who expose embarrassing business truths or false performance claims or economic malfeasance usually end up in prison camps.

So Chinese people typically invest their savings based on rumour, tips on social media or on whatever their family and friends are doing. Their investing tends to be short-term and irrational; many watch the stock ticker daily and adjust their investments accordingly. In recent weeks, many middle-class investors have seen their savings wiped out, and many will have borrowed money to invest in a "sure thing" that has just gone to dust.

But the larger question relates to the implications for the Communist Party rule in general. When China's stock markets were booming, the Communist media celebrated this as a sign of the superiority of the country's authoritarian state capitalist model of "socialism with Chinese characteristics." But when things are going very wrong, it is the party that is seen as accountable for the consequences.

The bottom line is that the Chinese middle class has been co-opted by the party to sacrifice their entitlements to citizenship, and to democratic freedoms and rights, in exchange for the promise of better living standards.

But if the Chinese economy continues to go south, it may dawn on 90 million largely urban, middle-class investors that the party is unable to keep up its side of the bargain.

If that were to happen, the prestige and legitimacy of Chinese President Xi Jinping's leadership could erode rapidly. This would have grave implications for the country's political and economic stability, as new voices emerge catering to the nationalist and populist yearnings of a people whose social values and aspirations are increasingly at odds with the country's political and judicial institutions.

And if the people lose faith in economic systems they associate with corruption, secrecy and mistrust, many Chinese might decide to never invest in the markets again.

A hard economic landing with resultant political and social chaos would be disastrous for China. And it would have a major impact on other trading countries, such as Canada, whose prosperity is increasingly dependent on China's stability and economic health.

Time and again, the Chinese Communist Party has shown surprising resilience in being able to preserve its political dominance and maintain national stability in the face of social and economic crises. It is probably in the best interests of billions of people that the government can somehow pull it off again.

Determined to shock world economics into a situation more favorable to China, the regime in Beijing suddenly devalued its currency in an effort to bump up its own export sales while making imported goods more expensive for Chinese citizens to buy. But while most central bankers understand that fiscal strength is largely dictated by bilateral fiscal strategies, China's closed system generates decisions following policies that are political, not economic.

China learns it can't control the laws of economics

THE GLOBE AND MAIL, 13 AUGUST 2015

CHINA'S AGGRESSIVE MOVE TO MANIPULATE THE value of its currency tells us two things: Its economy is in much deeper trouble than had been thought, and Beijing's crackdown on corruption is turning out to be a double-edged sword.

China stunned world markets this week by abruptly devaluing its currency 2 per cent on Tuesday, then letting it slide further on Wednesday, instantly rendering Canadian goods and services more expensive in China, making Chinese exports cheaper for Canadians to buy, and leaving our trade deficit even worse from a Canadian perspective.

The cheaper yuan also makes Chinese goods more competitive abroad than those of other Asian exporting countries. This will probably lead those countries to also devalue their currencies — more bad news for Canada. And imported oil will become more expensive in China, which has all sorts of commensurate impacts for China's airlines and manufacturers, global commodity prices and the Canadian economy in general.

We already knew things are not well with China's economy. Exports plummeted 8.3 per cent year-over-year in July; the manufacturing sector is badly underperforming expectations; and China's stock market is in crisis, increasingly dependent on government support that cannot be sustained indefinitely. But the surprise devaluation is a strong signal that the economy is in even worse shape than the Communist leadership had believed.

It is not a decision Beijing will have taken lightly. For one thing, it will surely lead to even more capital flight, Canada being a prime destination for Chinese citizens seeking a haven for their wealth. It will also discourage foreign investment in China; nobody wants to board a sinking ship.

This week's developments threaten the entire global economy. So what can China or even the World Bank or IMF do to turn this situation around?

Economist Friedrich Hayek wrote, "The curious task of economics is to demonstrate to men how little they really know about what they imagine they can design." But Mr. Hayek was a champion of classical liberal economics, and China's state capitalism operates quite differently. The bottom-line factor in China's economic decline seems tied to the political, not economic, policies of Xi Jinping's leadership since he became General Secretary of the Chinese Communist Party in 2012.

The hallmark of Mr. Xi's rule has been a massive clampdown on officials in government or state-owned enterprises who have accumulated great wealth beyond their very modest state salaries. Initially, this was seen as just another campaign to purge political factions that had been discomfited by Mr. Xi's assumption of power. After all, politicians on the outs in China are routinely convicted of corruption and sent to prison.

However, Mr. Xi's anti-corruption campaign is very popular with most people in China, and shows no signs of slowing down. But, ironically, the anti-corruption crusade meant to squeeze China's culture of business corruption is also squeezing China's economic growth.

Incarceration is a looming nightmare for the burgeoning ranks of Party elite whose families live beyond their legitimate means, and who have yet to "fall into the web," as the Chinese press puts it. Tranche after tranche of wealthy Communists in the state and military are being subject to confinement, torture, interrogation and the seizing of their assets. The Xi regime is even pressing foreign governments to deport corrupt Chinese officials who have sought refuge abroad — and are offering co-operative foreign governments a cut of the seized assets.

With the penalties for bribery, insider dealings, tax evasion and holding large sums of cash too high to risk being involved in many conventional Chinese business ventures, "political entrepreneurs" are finding it prudent to sit things out for the time being. And because many corrupt business networks have been decimated by the arrests of their key players, these will take some time to revive. Meanwhile, economic activity has slowed, and the national numbers look worse and worse.

For Xi Jinping's economic advisers, it's a classic Catch-22: In a state economic system where corruption is what oils the machine of business activity, how do you keep things going when the incentive of ill-gotten wealth is suddenly supplanted by the prospect of torture, prison and family ruin?

China's economic slowdown is not just due to economic factors; political moves also play a significant role. On the one hand, the Chinese political system is threatened by unchecked corruption on the part of the Communist political and business elite. On the other hand, people support the continued authoritarian rule of the Communist Party because it has been able to deliver high economic growth rates and a stronger nation.

China's closed-state capitalist political economy is just not sustainable without transparency, accountability and the genuine rule of law by an independent judiciary. Even Mr. Hayek would have to agree that the People's Republic of China is just as subject to the universal laws of economics as every other nation in the world.

The problem for the Chinese Communist Party is that, in the end, the liberal economies only sustain in liberal democracies.

As China parades its military hardware through Tiananmen Square, ostensibly to mark the 70th anniversary of the Second World War, it is staging a carefully calculated and executed show of power. Even the "true friends" guest list of state leaders is a message, touting anti-Western figures like Vladimir Putin, South Africa's Jacob Zuma, Pakistan's Mamnoon Hussain — but no leaders from the United States, Japan, Germany or Canada.

Who will march with China at Xi's parade?

THE GLOBE AND MAIL, 1 SEPTEMBER 2015

ON THURSDAY IN BEIJING, A MASSIVE military pageant will course through Tiananmen Square. For hours, thousands of crisply trained troops will march in formation as line after line of tanks, missiles and every other instrument of destruction, more than 500 in all, puts on a display meant to shock and awe.

Nobody will rain on this parade. To achieve a "military parade blue sky" on the day, the government has been restricting the use of vehicles and temporarily closed polluting industries for miles around. They also imposed new software on China's Great Firewall to enhance Internet censorship, which the Communist Party newspaper called an "upgrade for cyberspace sovereignty."

These steps, combined with the usual roundup of outspoken lawyers and human-rights proponents, attest to the importance that the party has placed on this show of its military might. To further mark the occasion, a large number of prisoners who served in the Communist military before their life of crime will be granted clemency and released from jail.

The pretext is the 70th anniversary of "victory of the war of resistance against Japanese aggression and the world's anti-fascist war" — also known as the Second World War. Of course, the huge contribution of Allied forces, the Chinese Nationalist Kuomintang (now in exile in Taiwan) and the U.S. atomic bombs to defeat the Japanese has been slighted in a new revisionist narrative that buttresses China's increasingly assertive expansionist strategy.

Many world leaders have been invited to watch from the Gate of Heavenly Peace overlooking Tiananmen Square. The Ministry of Foreign Affairs formally announced the list of China's "true friends" who will view the parade alongside the Communist leadership.

In a sign of China's spiralling dominance in East Asia, the President of South Korea will be a prominent participant. In sharp contrast, North Korea — whose Workers' Party had previously been characterized "as close as lips to teeth" to the Chinese Communist Party — is sending just a member of its Politburo. This startling gesture raises the question of how much longer South Korea will allow U.S. troops to be stationed there. Vietnam's President will also attend, but not leaders of Malaysia, the Philippines or other parties to the South China Sea territorial dispute.

The guest list comprises 30 state leaders, including Russia's Vladimir Putin, Jacob Zuma of South Africa and Pakistan's Mamnoon Hussain. But no leaders are attending from the United States, Japan, Germany or Canada.

With its invitation to the parade, Beijing is essentially asking countries: "Whose side are you on?" South Korea's and Vietnam's responses suggest how they see the future of the Sino-American power balance. On the other hand, the attendance by the President of the Czech Republic forms the sole exception to the European Union's reluctance to show up and symbolically affirm China's continuing rise in the global order.

This all comes at a time when the Communist Party is feeling less secure about its rule, given that China's economic institutions remain in serious, unprecedented crisis, and there have been surprising expressions of public anger over tragedies such as the Tianjin chemical explosion and even fundamentals such as food safety.

President Xi Jinping has responded with a crackdown on "Western influences," a consolidation of power for his office and an intense anti-corruption purge incarcerating and harshly interrogating more than 100,000 Communist officials, most associated with factions in China's security apparatus or military, or with loyalty to previous party strongmen Hu Jintao and Jiang Zemin.

However, the ferocity of this latest oppression has caught public attention, prompting a rare and intriguing admission in China's state media that "the scale of the resistance" to Mr. Xi's new policies "is beyond what could have been imagined."

This does not bode well, but don't expect the party to court the citizenry by moving toward democratic political institutions, a free press or an independent judiciary. Any shortcomings of China's governance will continue to be ascribed to the foreign-inspired moral failings of corrupted individual officials, not to any deficiencies in the political and economic system itself.

Over time, the regime's response will most certainly be more sabre-rattling assertions of nationalism, to rally the public behind Mr. Xi's leadership. Thursday's parade could be just the beginning of a new era in Chinese Communist militarism.

As the UK cozies up to Beijing, chasing richer trade relations, they sign $80-billion worth of economic agreements — including the folly of giving China a substantial stake in Britain's nuclear industry. Three decades earlier, then-PM Pierre Trudeau courted similar affinity with China. Premier Zhao Ziyang became the first Communist leader to address a joint session of Canada's Parliament, with PET enthusing "our bilateral relations have achieved such variety, depth and warmth". A few years later, Mr. Zhao was purged for supporting the Tiananmen Square democracy movement. He eventually died silenced and imprisoned.

Relations with China should hinge on more than short-term economic value

THE GLOBE AND MAIL, 26 OCTOBER 2015

LAST YEAR'S DECLARATION BY CHANCELLOR OF the Exchequer George Osborne that Britain would be China's "best partner in the West" has just been followed up by an extraordinary state visit to Britain by Chinese President Xi Jinping, one that led to the signing of agreements worth nearly $80-billion.

These deals controversially include giving China a substantial stake in Britain's nuclear industry as both an investor and contractor, and represent the most dramatically comprehensive push for Chinese investment by any Western country to date.

Because this has been at the expense of all other non-business considerations in relations with China, Britain has in effect significantly weakened the negotiating power of all other countries over such issues as human rights, cyberespionage, China's ambitions in the South China Sea and the many other concerns and threats occasioned by China's dramatic economic rise to power serving its nationalistic imperatives.

This begs the question whether Canada will follow suit with a similar "trade first" approach to China. In 2012, Justin Trudeau told CTV's Question Period that his support for the Chinese National Offshore Oil Corp.'s acquisition of Nexen, and for expanded future Chinese state investment in Canada, was at least partly because "obviously, my family has historical ties with China."

In the context of his time, Pierre Trudeau evidently felt that, despite his championing of the Charter of Rights and Freedoms for Canadians, people in the Third World were better suited to authoritarian dictatorships. Hence his close friendship with Cuba's Fidel Castro and his much expressed reverence for China's Chairman Mao Zedong.

In 1984, Chinese Premier Zhao Ziyang became the first Communist leader to address a joint session of Canada's Parliament. In his introductory remarks that day, then-prime minister Pierre Trudeau enthused that "our bilateral relations have achieved such variety, depth and warmth," and effused about the "most valued memory" of his 1973 visit to China, discussing politics with then-premier Zhou Enlai "far into the night." A few years later, Mr. Zhao was purged for supporting the Tiananmen Square democracy movement, and eventually died silenced and imprisoned under severe house arrest.

Later, Liberal prime minister Jean Chrétien followed a policy of "quiet diplomacy" with China on non-commercial matters, as urged by his Chinese interlocutors. This was designed ostensibly to better serve Canadian interests by insulating our economic initiatives in China from

Chinese politics. Mr. Chrétien's view was that China's integration into global regimes such as the World Trade Organization would eventually lead Beijing to adopt democratic institutions and independent rule of law.

In fact, Canada's share of China's imports actually declined over the Chrétien years, and Beijing's human-rights record continues to deteriorate. Amnesty International reports that, since July of this year, 245 human-rights lawyers and activists have been targeted by the Chinese government. Incredibly, this year's winner of the Confucius Peace Prize is Zimbabwe's appalling President Robert Mugabe.

Clearly, "quiet diplomacy" has had no discernible positive impact, but rather functions as tacit consent for egregious Chinese regime behaviour. Canada should have no further part of it. We simply lose the respect of the Chinese regime if we do not speak out honestly and constructively about our concerns over China's human-rights violations, support for rogue dictators, cyberespionage and Beijing's underhanded attempts to subvert the decisions of Canadian political leaders in order to further China's state interests.

The Trudeau family's "historical ties with China" will undoubtedly provide the younger Mr. Trudeau with a strong basis for engaging the Chinese leadership. We can expect that he will make a state visit to China an early foreign-policy foray, followed by a return visit by Mr. Xi to Canada, accompanied by a large business delegation with billions to invest.

Willingness to seriously engage the once-isolated China was a positive hallmark of past Liberal governments, from Pierre Trudeau on, but the dynamics of that relationship have changed considerably since that era. It would be negligent to not appreciate the threat to Canadian sovereignty and interests posed by Beijing's non-democratic, nationalistic, expansionist Leninist politics.

Canada should not blithely follow Britain's example and try to compete for the title of China's "best partner in the West." We must be mindful of more than just the short-term economic benefits of unconditional engagement with China.

Having a new government in Ottawa is a time for fresh beginnings, and our new regime should consider its approach to China very carefully in light of Canadian interests and values.

This essay about China lifting its one-child limit draws on Burton's personal past of living in China. He saw first-hand how people got around strict Party doctrines by having "invisible" children born secretly, beyond the government quotas. Permanently consigned to the margins of society, these children did not officially exist as citizens of the Chinese state.

Goodbye to the age of China's 'little emperors'

THE GLOBE AND MAIL, 30 OCTOBER 2015

IN A MOVE THAT WILL FIND great favour with families across China, the Communist regime is easing its controversial one-child limit and will allow couples to have two children.

When China's leaders imposed strict childbirth limits in 1980, they were tacitly admitting that economic growth in the first 30 years of Communist rule was so poor that, unless the population were controlled by the state, it would instead be controlled brutally and naturally through famine.

I remember well, from my own lean student days in China during the 1970s, the strict rationing of grain and other foodstuffs. How times have changed. Today, China can afford to compensate for shortfalls in its own grain production, and has been a net importer of food for more than a decade.

The one-child policy — which required that most citizens get permission from the state to have a child — came into effect not long after the death of Chairman Mao Zedong. Under Mao, the Chinese Communist Party encouraged families to have as many children as possible because of his belief that population growth empowered the country. Over the quarter-century of his rule, China's population ballooned from around 540 million in 1949 to 940 million in 1976.

Today, China faces the inverse perils of a rapidly aging population. By 2030, it is estimated there will be one person drawing a pension for every two working taxpayers, so the population pendulum must urgently start swinging the other way or the social effects will again be dire.

The easing of family-planning laws was much anticipated, and long overdue.

In the early years, the consequences of quotas on pregnancies were very harsh. Women who sought to conceal unplanned pregnancies were often subject to the horror of late-term abortions. Abandonment and infanticide of baby girls became common because, under Chinese cultural norms and in the absence of social welfare measures, it was sons who would carry on the family name and care for their parents in old age. Government campaigns encouraging families to cherish daughters, and attempts to restrict the use of ultrasound examinations to determine fetus gender, largely failed for this reason.

The subsequent lopsided demographic ratio of males to females has made it difficult for poor young men to find wives, and led many frustrated young bachelors to criminal gang activity in response to the social shame of becoming a so-called "barren branch" on the family tree. The kidnapping and sale of young women, some even brought in from border countries such as North Korea, has been an ongoing problem, not to mention China's rampant spread of prostitution.

Moreover, the policy led to the creation of a subclass of "invisible" children, born secretly outside the quotas. Such children cannot legalize their registry in urban areas, attend school, qualify for social welfare benefits or even apply for passports to seek a less shadowy life abroad. Millions live a Kafkaesque life, permanently consigned to the margins of society, because they do not officially exist as citizens of the Chinese state.

A further legacy of this is that the large number of Chinese children adopted into Canadian families, bringing joy to couples who yearn to be parents, are nearly all little girls. China has orphanages full of them, waiting for good homes abroad.

State enforcement of the one-child policy, however, has always been inconsistent. Ethnic minorities were largely exempted to lessen their discontent, and in recent years there was a loosening in urban areas that were experiencing population decline. As well, these family-planning regulations became another pretext for official corruption through fines or bribes extracted from couples who could afford to essentially buy permission to have a second child or even a third.

Perhaps the greatest benefit of the policy change will be sociological. Under the one-child policy, most children are overindulged by two parents and four grandparents. They have no brothers or sisters, cousins, or uncles and aunts. All the expectations of the generations fall onto their young shoulders, and the pressure to succeed can be crushing and character-distorting. Moreover, these "little emperors" tend to grow up with an exaggerated sense of self-importance and often lack the social sensibilities necessary to a civil society.

The termination of this policy is a rare piece of good news out of China, and should be welcomed. It's likely that Chinese couples with only one child will be turning in early tonight.

THE JUSTIN TRUDEAU ERA

His new government hoping to negotiate free trade with China, Prime Minister Justin Trudeau prepares to lead a major trade delegation to Beijing. This piece discusses the perils of pursuing such agreements with a country that expects unfettered access to markets and asset acquisitions, while greatly restricting how Canadian companies could compete for business in China.

Trudeau's dance with the dragon: China must give as much as it takes

THE GLOBE AND MAIL, 13 JANUARY 2016

THE NEWS THAT PRIME MINISTER JUSTIN Trudeau will lead a high-level trade mission to China this spring signals that his government intends to put stronger engagement with China at the forefront of its economic game plan. Having a deal in place before the next election could be a cornerstone of this strategy, but it won't be easy.

Australia and China finally achieved a free-trade deal last month, but it took 21 rounds of negotiations over more than 10 years — and the agreement remains controversial in Australia. For Canada, the question is whether we can negotiate something with China that will be of net benefit to Canada and does not require us to abandon principled commitments to uphold human rights and freedoms, here and throughout the world.

Interestingly, in 2014, China's newly arrived ambassador to Canada, Luo Zhaohui, said that a Canadian-Chinese free-trade pact should be a Canadian national priority. Seeing as China already has extensive free access to our markets and enjoys a huge trade surplus with Canada, one wonders what Beijing hopes to achieve with such an agreement.

The ambassador also urged Canada to roll back "negative" foreign investment rules that former prime minister Stephen Harper's government implemented in 2012, around the time it was considering approval of the China National Offshore Oil Corp.'s $15-billion acquisition of Canadian oil company Nexen. (Ottawa did ultimately approve the purchase.)

What Beijing wants is no restrictions on Chinese state investment in Canada, with no obligation to allow Canadian investment the same access in China. Consider the swift replacement of Nexen's Canadian CEO Kevin Reinhart with a Communist Party cadre (despite Beijing's earlier promise to maintain Nexen's Canadian management), or the years-long controversy over Chinese mining concerns in Canada's North bringing in Chinese miners on the absurd basis that they could not find local Mandarin speakers to apply for the jobs.

China wants its acquisitions in Canada to be fully integrated into China's supply chain, and all revenue generated by them — right down to miners' salaries — to benefit the Chinese state in every aspect. Mr. Luo also wants Ottawa to let Chinese state firms fully participate in constructing the Northern Gateway pipeline, in accordance, naturally, with Chinese environmental, labour and ethical standards that fall far short of Canadian benchmarks.

Meanwhile, polls by Canada's Asia-Pacific Foundation show that nearly half of Canadians oppose free trade with China, and more than three-quarters don't want state-owned Chinese firms buying out Canadian companies.

Mr. Trudeau's government is feeling pressure to show it is taking steps to address Canada's economic downturn and the growing federal debt; they want to be able to tout a free-trade deal with China as the road to Canada's economic revival. The worry is that, under such political pressure, Canadian negotiators will commit to a deal that will serve China's interests much more than ours.

Certainly the Canada-China Foreign Investment Promotion and Protection Agreement (FIPA) that came into effect in 2014 appears to fall into this category. Canada is constrained by its terms to protect Chinese investment from any negative impact of foreign investment, environmental or labour regulations that may be enacted by Ottawa or by provincial governments after 2014.

But Canada gets little reciprocal protection, given China's lack of transparent and enforceable business regulations and law. It remains to be seen whether FIPA leads to increasing Canada's share in Chinese markets, or fairer resolution of contract disputes over protection of intellectual property, proprietary manufacturing processes and so on.

As we have been reminded by the run of stock-market turmoil, China's economy is underperforming expectations, and in 2016, it is likely Beijing will continue to devalue the renminbi/yuan, making Canadian products even less competitive in China. Since slowing growth rates really do threaten China's political stability, one wonders whether, under these circumstances, Beijing would genuinely be prepared to further open its market to the kinds of products and services in which Canada has clear comparative advantage. Canadian banks, securities and insurance firms are currently subject to highly onerous restrictions on their Chinese operations, severely constraining their ability to compete against state firms for the same business.

Any credible free-trade agreement has to have give and take on both sides, but the asymmetrical power relationship between the political economies of our two countries has in the past led to a lot more take than give on the Chinese side. Before Canada signs on the dotted line, it is paramount to our national interest that any agreement with China be intensely scrutinized, without regard to political considerations, to ensure there is a fair measure of net benefit for Canada.

There is no question that Canada needs to be doing more trade with China to sustain Canadian national prosperity in the years and decades ahead. But where do we draw the line on the political, non-trade conditions that the Communist regime will almost certainly impose on Canada in return? And to what extent are we prepared to offer Beijing economic and therefore political leverage if our economy becomes more and more dependent on the vagaries of Chinese state investment?

Before they give us what we ask, the Chinese side will inevitably insist that Canada show "friendship" to the Chinese regime by not engaging on Canadians' concerns over allegations of human-rights abuse in any meaningful way, and not pressing too hard on consular cases such as that of Vancouver native Kevin Garratt, a Christian who has been jailed since August, 2014, without any due process of law.

The bottom line on enhancing our relations with China is whether, in our pursuit of the economic justice of fair trade, we have to largely abandon Canada's proud commitment to political and social justice.

Despite — or maybe because of — Canadians' skepticism about forging closer relations with China, the federal government strangely gave less than 24 hours' notice of a surprise official visit by China's Foreign Minister for a "foreign ministers' dialogue". Ottawa feels more trade with China is crucial to Canada's economic growth, but this piece argues that Canada must keep its eyes wide open, and tread carefully.

Trade with China never comes free

THE GLOBE AND MAIL, 2 JUNE 2016

WEDNESDAY'S SURPRISE "OFFICIAL VISIT" TO CANADA by Chinese Foreign Minister Wang Yi, disclosed by Ottawa less than 24 hours earlier, underscores the Liberal government's intent to intensify relations with China radically, regardless of Canadian public opposition or security concerns.

Foreign Affairs Minister Stéphane Dion said Mr. Wang was here for the previously unannounced "inaugural Canada-China Foreign Affairs Ministers' Dialogue, which is an important building block in our relationship with China" and to discuss "how to expand our strategic partnership for the benefit of Canadians."

Since the Liberals were elected on a platform that included revamping Canada's relationship with China, Prime Minister Justin Trudeau's policy mandarins have been preparing for enhanced engagement with

Beijing, including negotiating a free-trade deal and opening Canada's natural-resources sector to high levels of Chinese state investment.

But there has been no public consultation on this major policy shift, and while corporate interests are lobbying for more trade opportunities, public opinion remains skeptical of Mr. Trudeau's enthusiasm for China. The Prime Minister is expected to travel to China in August, laying the groundwork for a renewed relationship with Beijing before the September G20 meeting in Hangzhou.

China plays hardball in trade talks, and there is speculation Beijing wants Ottawa to show its commitment to any new relationship by promising to approve the Northern Gateway pipeline. That would allow Chinese President Xi Jinping to make a state visit to Canada, accompanied by Chinese state enterprise officials with tens of billions of investment deals in hand. Beijing has been clear that a free-trade deal is contingent on Canada building the pipeline from Alberta and developing port facilities for giant tankers plying the tricky straits off the B.C. coast. This would require strong unilateral government action overriding the concerns of Canadians, notably First Nations worried about the environmental effects of such an energy corridor.

Despite Mr. Trudeau's intentions about straight talk on issues of concern, the truth is that China dictates "no-go" zones as the cost of its state investment. For example, Britain could renew relations with China only after agreeing to end high-level meetings with the Dalai Lama. No less will be demanded of Ottawa. Any Canadian talk about human rights, or China harassing people in Canada perceived to be hostile to the regime, or increasing cyberattacks and espionage, or Chinese expansion in the South China Sea, is dismissed by Beijing as, absurdly, "hurting the feelings of the Chinese people," thereby disinclining state firms to trade and invest in Canada.

Then there is the alarming extent to which China has infiltrated Canada's government and its bureaucracy, an issue raised by former CSIS director Richard Fadden in an interview with CBC's As It Happens in April. Ottawa must address this threat with more seriousness of purpose.

A report last year by the Institute for Research on Public Policy bemoaned the "negativity" of Canadian public opinion regarding China, noting a wide gap between experts and the public in understanding the country. The report urged Canada to "deal with China not as we might wish it to be, but as an evolving social, political and economic system with values and institutions different from our own."

Last fall, a government transition document urged the Liberals to initiate a "national conversation" about "informing public opinion about the critical importance of China to Canada's future prosperity" and "addressing negative opinions hindering Canada's interests." We shall soon see if this is the direction the government will go to neutralize Canadians' deep concerns about human rights in China.

China represents less than 4 per cent of Canadian exports, so the two countries could do a lot more trade, but whether a free-trade deal would benefit Canada is contingent on its terms and implementation. It could simply make our trade deficit with China even wider, with no significant opening of the Chinese market to Canadian commodities and services.

Ottawa's quandary is that all things are definitely not equal in the asymmetrical power relationship between Canada and China. On what terms do we further engage with China? Canadians want to know what our government's bottom line is for compromise on Canadian values in Canada-China relations.

On the eve of Prime Minister Justin Trudeau's official visit to China, at a time of prickly relations between Ottawa and Beijing, this commentary observes how much has changed since then–Prime Minister Jean Chrétien led a Team Canada trade mission to China 20 years earlier.

Visit to China a tricky one for Trudeau

THE GLOBE AND MAIL, 24 AUGUST 2016

WHEN PRIME MINISTER JEAN CHRÉTIEN LED a Team Canada mission to China in 1998, he was permitted to deliver a speech at Beijing's Tsinghua University. Although it did not get reported in the Chinese media, Mr. Chrétien was able to utter a single sentence (drafted by myself, a political officer in Canada's Beijing embassy at the time) to mollify those in Canada who felt he was too soft with Chinese officials on human rights.

"I would be less than frank," Mr. Chrétien said, "if I did not say directly to you that many Canadians are disturbed when we hear of people being arrested or in prison for expressing political views different from the government."

As Prime Minister Justin Trudeau heads to China on Aug. 30 for a five-day visit prior to the Group of 20 meeting in Hangzhou, there is no way he will be allowed to deliver even such a highly nuanced sentiment at a university or any other public venue. In today's China, democracy and human rights are concepts too sensitive to be mentioned by a visiting Western leader.

Ottawa's press release announcing the visit said Mr. Trudeau "will strive for a closer, more balanced relationship between Canada and China." He has his work cut out.

Canada has some serious issues that the Prime Minister needs to resolve with China's leaders. For example, we face annual losses of $2-billion in export revenue as a result of Beijing's move to severely tighten regulations on Sept. 1 that will effectively halt imports of Canadian canola seeds. There is no scientific rationale for this restrictive measure; Canada is just competing too well against China's growing stockpile of unsold domestic rapeseed.

Another concern is Beijing's refusal to allow Canada consular access to Canadians of Hong Kong origin who travel to China. There are 300,000 Canadians resident in Hong Kong and Mr. Trudeau has famously stated that "a Canadian is a Canadian is a Canadian."

For its part, China demands that Canada retract its support of an international tribunal's ruling that Beijing's claim to 85 per cent of the South China Sea violates the UN Convention on the Law of the Sea, to which China is party.

Beijing also wants Ottawa to repatriate Chinese Communist cadres it says have fled to Canada with ill-gotten gains, even though China has provided little evidence of alleged offences, and we know that such people would be subject to torture in the course of the horrific internal investigation procedure called *shuanggui*.

Then there's the moral elephant in the room: How Mr. Trudeau can square enhanced economic engagement against (a) China's egregious human rights record, (b) China's enabling support for dangerous dictatorships from North Korea to Zimbabwe, and (c) China's aggressive expansionist policies, particularly in the South China Sea.

This file has never been easy. In the 1970s, Prime Minister Pierre Trudeau, in extraordinary naiveté, admired the Communist leaders of his time, Mao Zedong and Zhou Enlai, as good and wise rulers dedicated to revolutionary social justice. This as millions of Chinese were being subject to torture in the name of Marxist ideological remoulding, with untold numbers left to die in the Great Proletarian Cultural Revolution.

By the 1990s, Mr. Chrétien reached out to Chinese Premier Li Peng — a key player in the violent suppression of the 1989 Tiananmen Movement — on the basis that economic engagement with the West would lead China to a democratic transition. To this end, he agreed to give tacit consent to China's human rights violations by a "going-through-the-motions" engagement of China on human rights behind closed doors.

Now, our Prime Minister wants to build a new relationship on a palatable moral foundation. Unfortunately, under General Secretary Xi Jinping the democracy and human rights train has left the station and won't be coming back on his watch.

The increasingly insecure regime's respect for human rights keeps deteriorating, with more reports of "disappearances" of respected lawyers and severe constraints being imposed on freedom of speech and freedom of conscience. There is a *fin de siècle* mood in China as the official propaganda legitimizing Mr. Xi's power is increasingly removed from the values of the populace, the economy falters, and more and more state resources are allocated to "maintaining stability" by ever-stricter Internet censorship and more power for the secret police. These are scary times in China.

Canadians deserve a better and more Canadian-values-based approach to China. An "old wine in new bottles" policy with China will not work, and history will not judge Justin Trudeau well if this is the way the government chooses to go.

In examining the contemporary scourge of fentanyl, this article draws an ironic parallel to the 19th-century Opium War and how Hong Kong came to be a British holding.

Enlisting Beijing to help stop fentanyl exports won't be easy

THE GLOBE AND MAIL, 6 DECEMBER 2016

SO THE RCMP AND CHINA'S MINISTRY of Public Security have announced they will work together to combat the surge of fentanyl and other opioids flowing from China into Canada.

The need for action is undoubtedly urgent. Fentanyl has been the instrument of death for hundreds of heroin and cocaine users in Canada, and CSIS intelligence suggests almost all the fentanyl comes from small synthetic chemical factories all over China.

Canada is unable to suppress the demand for it, and it is impossible to stop fentanyl from relentlessly arriving by mail in small quantities. So the only measure left is to get Chinese police to put a stop to the killer chemical from leaving the factories where it is manufactured.

For students of Chinese history, there's irony in Canada's demand on moral grounds that China suppress the export of a synthetic opioid. In the 19th century, opium addiction in China was rampant, and the opium was almost entirely imported into China from British India. In response, China implemented the world's earliest drug laws, making the sale, import and consumption of opium illegal.

In Victorian England, however, opium eating was quite legal, and as all Chinese schoolchildren are now taught, Britain's refusal to respect Chinese law and ban the export of opium into China was a signal event in Chinese history. When the Chinese government destroyed a large quantity of illegal British opium by dumping it off the docks of Canton into the sea, Britain declared war. China's devastating defeat in that war resulted in it being forced to cede the Island of Hong Kong to Britain in perpetuity under the humiliating conditions of the 1842 Treaty of Nanking. The Opium War is considered to mark the modern era in China, its ultimate resolution being the expulsion of the Western imperialists after the Communist victory in 1949.

This history could explain the reported lack of enthusiasm by Chinese police to respond vigorously to Canada's request that Beijing close down fentanyl production and export. China doesn't have a significant fentanyl problem domestically. It deals with the problem by executing drug smugglers and dealers and by imprisoning illegal-drug users for a program of forced rehabilitation that they or their families pay for. In a police state that keeps close tabs on all citizens, this policy is relatively effective.

Beijing is unlikely to aggressively suppress this lucrative export for the sake of international public interest alone. Undoubtedly China's fentanyl manufacturers are issuing the necessary bribes to keep their operations free from government harassment. Moreover, Chinese culture suggests police there are only likely to actively suppress fentanyl exports if Ottawa offers an incentive to do so.

Start with money. The Chinese government would likely require that their investigation into fentanyl exports be generously funded by Canada. This is not an altogether out-of-the-way demand, as Beijing would expect that any proceeds of crime seized through the arrests of Canadian distributors should subsidize its own fentanyl-export suppression costs.

But another condition of this pact could be more co-operation with Chinese authorities tracking down Chinese nationals in Canada who Beijing wants to see returned to China.

These are hard times for Canada — with hard choices. Not only is the federal government eyeing freer trade with China as a way to insulate Canada's economy from the ravages of an isolationist Trump presidency, Ottawa also hopes to restore the purity of our illegal heroin and cocaine from deadly Chinese fentanyl by looking to Chinese Communist goodwill and trust.

We are probably better off looking to non-Chinese solutions for both.

On the 20th anniversary of Hong Kong being returned to China, this article discusses Beijing's broken promises as it demolished longstanding institutions that defined Hong Kong's function and freedoms. Readers may note a sobering parallel to Donald Trump's dismantling of U.S. government agencies and systems after his return to the presidency in 2025.

Hong Kong, and the litany of Beijing's betrayal

THE GLOBE AND MAIL, 30 JUNE 2017

CHINESE PRESIDENT XI JINPING'S VISIT TO Hong Kong, marking 20 years since it was returned to China from British rule, has been met by a fierce security lockdown, hordes of protesters, thousands of armed police and the arrests of political activists.

On this milestone anniversary, Hong Kong is reeling as it is dragged deeper into a status whose blueprint is a string of broken promises by Beijing.

Hong Kong's modern history has been unorthodox, a free-wheeling but Westernized speck on a decidedly undemocratic regional map. It had been ceded to the U.K. in 1842 after China lost a war that was waged to defend Britain's continuing exports of India's opium (after China had outlawed its use).

Fast-forward 146 years to July 1, 1997, and a surreal open-air pageant with the President of China and members of the Communist Party Politburo onstage. A tropical downpour had just drenched the jam-packed parade square. Prince Charles, Margaret Thatcher, final Hong Kong Governor Chris Patten and young new Prime Minister Tony Blair glumly watched goose-stepping soldiers of the People's Liberation Army. When the red and yellow flag of the People's Republic of China was raised to replace the Union Jack, the euphoric crowd let loose a jubilance Hong Kong had never known.

The future seemed exciting. In a Joint Declaration that set the terms of reversion to Chinese sovereignty, Beijing promised Hong Kong's social and economic systems would remain unchanged, and rights and freedoms — including those of the press, of association, of correspondence, of strike, of academic research and of religious belief — protected. China promised "one country, two systems" and "no change for 50 years," and said "Hong Kong people would govern Hong Kong." That meant Hong Kong would be governed by locally elected leaders.

A subdued Prince Charles sounded like he didn't believe his own farewell remarks: "We have no doubt that Hong Kong people can run Hong Kong, as the Joint Declaration promises . . . and that faithful implementation of the Declaration is key to Hong Kong's continued success . . . I wish you all a successful transition, and a prosperous and peaceful future."

Communist leaders have occasionally repeated that democratic institutions and rule of law remained the end game for post-Mao China (though always with the caveat that these goals could not be realized immediately due to historical, cultural and developmental factors).

Canada endorsed the Joint Declaration at the UN, expecting Beijing to eventually comply with international norms of democratic governance. In 1998, China signed the UN's International Covenant on Civil and Political Rights, giving assurance (false, as we now know) that China was moving in this direction.

But in 2013, Xi Jinping became President and began making statements explicitly renouncing such political ideals as constitutionalism, freedom of the press, judicial independence, and speech and assembly. He said they were incompatible with sustained Communist Party rule in China. One of the Party's official newspapers condemned these principles as "a ticket to hell" for China.

China nixed any notions about universal suffrage in Hong Kong, instead introducing pro-Party curriculum in schools, intimidating independent media and illegally relocating several Hong Kong residents deemed hostile to the Beijing regime to the mainland. This betrayal has been met with public outrage and massive protests in the streets, including one in 2014 that occupied some districts of downtown Hong Kong for three months.

More and more young Hong Kongers are now demanding genuine autonomy, if not outright independence, from China, renouncing their Mandarin-based Chinese-ness in favour of a localized Cantonese Hong Kong identity. When some of this new generation were recently democratically elected to the local legislature, China's No. 3 state leader Zhang Dejiang warned that Hong Kong must be governed by "patriots who sincerely support China's sovereignty."

Politically, things are volatile and dangerously uncertain in Hong Kong, and it matters a lot to Canada. There are 300,000 Canadian citizens in Hong Kong, and half a million Canadians of Hong Kong origin reside in Canada. That's a strong Canadian connection for a place with just seven million residents.

So far, Chinese troops in Hong Kong have stayed in their barracks. For how much longer is anyone's guess. In June 1989, observers pondered similar questions about Tiananmen Square.

As Canadian officials remain tight-lipped about ongoing trade talks with China, this piece looks behind the curtain and finds that Chinese officials are calling the shots and playing the gullible Canadians for chumps. As Canada tries to play it straight, Beijing demands that Canada simply concede that "China is the future, and sustaining Canada's economic growth means Ottawa should acquiesce to Beijing's 'distinctive' domestic governance and strategic aspirations abroad."

Oh Canada: The roaring silence around trade talks with China

HONG KONG FREE PRESS, 26 AUGUST 2017

AS CANADIANS DIGEST A STREAM OF news and punditry about NAFTA renegotiations, there's another trade relationship — possibly more consequential for our future — that's being forged in comparative silence.

The second China-Canada Foreign Ministers Dialogue was recently held in Beijing, with Canada's Chrystia Freeland sitting down with her counterpart Wang Yi to "explore ways to further consolidate Canada-China ties," as Xinhua news agency put it. Upcoming Canada-China trade talks topped the agenda.

But despite anxiety in Canada over China's demands in any new deal, and what's at stake should Canada dramatically increase our trade with the Chinese, we know little about what was even discussed. Freeland flew home with no post-meeting news conference. No communiqué was issued.

Given the shocking spectacle that crowned last year's edition of this dialogue when Wang arrogantly berated a Canadian journalist who asked about China's human rights record, many might suspect the secrecy is Beijing's precondition to any further talks. Based on my past experience as counsellor at the Canadian embassy in Beijing, I find this quite likely.

Canada a 'friend of China?'

When John McCallum, now Canada's ambassador to China, was a federal cabinet minister, he was a champion of expanding connections between Canada and China, and doing it on Chinese terms. McCallum, who was at the recent meetings with Freeland, evidently buys in to Beijing's "friend of China" platitude.

He apparently accepts the Chinese Foreign Ministry line that China is the future, and sustaining Canada's economic growth means Ottawa should acquiesce to Beijing's "distinctive" domestic governance and strategic aspirations abroad.

As Justin Trudeau himself said in 2012: "We deceive ourselves by thinking that trade with Asia can be squeezed into the 20th-century mould. China, for one, sets its own rules and will continue to do so because it can. China has a game plan. There is nothing inherently sinister about that."

McCallum, the cabinet minister, likely would have agreed, even if turning a blind eye from human rights abuse in China is tacit consent of arbitrary imprisonment, torture, suffering and death.

But McCallum, the ambassador, is subordinate to his former junior cabinet colleague Freeland, who is thought to have a more textured and sophisticated grasp of Communist regimes and how to promote Canadian interests in discussions with the Chinese.

Chinese media had details

Her priorities for relations with China might not sit well with McCallum, and there could be tensions between them that Beijing will try to exploit to further its own goals with Canada.

If Ottawa was reticent to reveal what was said at the meeting, the Chinese media was more forthcoming. *China Daily* reported that Wang said "China and Canada should maintain high-level exchanges and exchanges at other various levels, promote the construction of a China-Canada free trade zone and expand anti-corruption and law enforcement cooperation."

Canada has a problem with this last point, which implies extraditing Chinese nationals from Canada despite our concerns over China's lack of due process of law and extensive use of the death penalty.

Seasoned China-watchers wonder if the Prime Minister's Office told Freeland to avoid engaging her Chinese interlocutors on issues of concern to the Canadian public, such as the disappearance of Liu Xia, the widow of the Nobel laureate Liu Xiaobo; or the ongoing (17 months and counting) imprisonment of B.C. wine exporter John Chang over what China calls a "customs valuation dispute" but which may really be about refusing demands for payoffs.

Canadians troubled by Chinese human rights record

Canadians also deplore China's violent persecution of ethnic minorities, people of faith and the lawyers who seek to defend them under Chinese law.

Opinion polls, along with Ottawa's own consultations with Canadians, suggest public alarm over Chinese trade practices, forced transfer of intellectual property and Beijing's growing influence in Canada.

There's also deep concern about precedents that include Chinese enterprises owning Canada's natural resource enterprises, and Beijing's demand to use imported Chinese labour on Chinese-directed projects within Canada.

Of course, despite any public apprehension, the PMO is under pressure from Canada's China-related major corporations to press ahead with free trade anyway.

From her past writings and statements, we know that Freeland is unlikely to support unconditional expansion of relations with China at the cost of sacrifice of the Canadian values she has so strongly upheld.

But her silence following her first trip to China as foreign affairs minister is both deafening and troubling.

With the Chinese Communist Party's Congress behind him, President Xi Jinping's authority was now absolute, having eliminated term limits and enshrining himself as the sole legitimate interpreter of Chinese Marxism. Next up: Dealing with the rest of the world.

As Xi sets his sights on the world, the ruse is dispensed with

TORONTO STAR, 26 OCTOBER 2017

WHEN THE CHINESE COMMUNIST PARTY'S 19TH Congress ended on Tuesday, President Xi Jinping emerged, as planned, with a steely new grip on power.

Having been enshrined in the Party Constitution as the sole legitimate interpreter of Chinese Marxism for the "new era," Xi's political authority in China is absolute. Now he can concentrate on the rest of the world.

Held every five years, a recurring theme of this year's Congress was China's historical resentment against, and future redress of, the West. Communist officials chafe at China's humiliating defeat by the British in the Opium War of 1840, and subsequent Western and Japanese imperialistic incursions. China's past characterization as "the sick man of Asia" was cited many times during the Congress.

But now Xi has assumed "the mandate of history" to implement the "magnificent plan" realizing the "Chinese dream of glorious Chinese national restoration" by 2050. Proceeding from 2020, this plan is divided into two 15-year parts. By 2035, China will be fully developed and technologically advanced. It will then embark on taking its rightful place as the world's unassailable economic and cultural leader, playing "an important role in the history of humanity."

Speaking without compromise, Xi envisioned a post-2050 new world order he dubs "the community of the common destiny of humankind," which the People's Daily newspaper allows is "superior to Western mainstream international relations theory." In that world, America's downward spiral under Donald Trump continues unabated, and with it the end of Western liberal internationalism based on democracy and the values of human rights and citizenship. Indeed, Xi hailed China as a model for "nations that want to speed up their development while preserving their independence."

State authoritarianism and global power politics is how Beijing sees the rise to dominance playing out. Human rights and multilateral co-operation have no part in it. It seems that clock is already ticking, as China also announced the termination of its senior-level human rights dialogue with Australia.

China craves international affirmation and respect. Night after night, throughout the week-long Congress, Central Chinese TV news played clips of leaders around the world expressing support for the Congress, including a brief and heavily edited interview with Canada's Jean Chrétien.

From conference documents, it is clear that Xi Jinping's "socialism with Chinese characteristics for a new era" means more tightening of political debate and restriction of foreign influence. The indications are that China will further close its markets to foreign business in favour of more aggressive championing of "China first;" that "non-Chinese" religions (especially Islam and Christianity) will be further suppressed; and that policies toward China's non-Han peoples are changing from ethnic accommodation to hard assimilation into the great "China nation" — a tragedy for the great Uyghur and Tibetan civilizations already weak and struggling for survival under Beijing's suppression.

How sustainable is this grand plan? The danger in concentrating all power in his own hands is that while Xi is praised to the skies in state media for all China's successes, he will also be held accountable for anything that goes wrong. It remains to be seen if the general population is truly prepared to sacrifice Chinese democracy and social justice for the promise of a Communist elite-led rise to pre-eminent global power 33 years hence.

The Congress did have some positive outcomes for the Chinese people. The Party promises to eliminate poverty by 2020, making China a beacon of hope for Third World nations. Xi also spoke of doing away with *shuanggui*, the brutal interrogation and torture technique reserved for Party officials. Devised in the 1930s to deal with traitors, spies and the ideologically impure, it has more recently come to include anyone who opposes Xi's dictatorship.

Of course, torture is standard practice in Chinese police stations and prisons. Therein lies the conundrum. In capitals around the world, a main take-away from Congress is Beijing's now openly brazen contempt for any liberties, at a time when nations are jockeying to engage China on a presumption of mutual respect for human rights.

With Canada eyeing free trade with Chinese, our Parliament just adopted Bill C-267 — the "Magnitsky Act" — which bars entry by, and forbids Canadians from financially engaging with, foreign nationals who are complicit in torture or extrajudicial killings of anyone who defends or promotes human rights and freedoms, such as the right to a fair trial or democratic elections. As Canada proceeds to identify Russians and Venezuelans for the Magnitsky list, there are already many Chinese Communist officials who instantly meet the criteria.

It will be interesting to see if their names are added to the list before or after trade negotiations.

The PMO announces, on short notice, a trip by Prime Minister Justin Trudeau to China, where he will pursue his determination to establish "a progressive trade agenda" and "frank dialogue on human rights". This column examines the ridiculous basis of such delusionary expectations.

Does Trudeau really believe trade with China is 'free'?

THE GLOBE AND MAIL, 1 DECEMBER 2017

LAST SUNDAY AFTERNOON, WHILE CANADIANS SETTLED in for the Grey Cup game, the Prime Minister's Office announced that Justin Trudeau will fly to Beijing this weekend for talks about "a progressive trade agenda" as well as "frank dialogue on human rights issues like good governance, freedom of speech and the rule of law." Frank dialogue on human rights? The federal Liberals are dreaming if they think skeptical Canadians will buy the official line on Mr. Trudeau's sudden visit to China.

Beijing has made clear it will not abide by aspirations of a "progressive trade agenda." Inserting clauses on human rights, the environment or regulatory transparency into free-trade talks is a non-starter. This regime demands that Canadian companies operating in China transfer technology and intellectual-property rights to their Chinese state partners.

A free-trade agreement (FTA) won't change that. No such "progressive" conditions appear in FTAs with New Zealand or Australia. Why would Beijing give a minor global player such as Canada special consideration?

Ottawa's report this year on the "Public consultations on a possible Canada-China FTA" has a long list of concerns cited by Canadian businesses who have had arbitrary taxes, import duties and "new" internal regulations imposed on them as their Chinese state partners squeezed them out of the Chinese market. The report strongly contradicts Mr. Trudeau's optimism that a China FTA will benefit Canada and should be taken seriously.

Beijing is unyielding that non-economic factors have no place in trade deals. If Canada wants enhanced access to China's market, it must toe Beijing's line on non-contact with Tibet's Dalai Lama; stay silent about threats to democracy in Hong Kong or Taiwan; drop objections to China's development of military facilities in international waters of the South China Sea; and submit to Chinese espionage in Canada and ever-increasing reports of aggressive menacing of Canadian citizens of Chinese origin to get them to serve the interests of the "motherland."

So, what more does China hope to get in an FTA? It already has excellent access to Canadian markets, thanks to low Canadian tariffs under the WTO, and Canada's fair and transparent import and investment regimes. Will Ottawa cave to demands of opening our energy and mining sectors to unfettered acquisition by Chinese state firms, if it will not lead to Canada getting reciprocal access to Chinese assets (which it won't)?

Moreover, the supposed benefits to Canada of free trade are underpinned by Beijing's rhetoric on "building trust." There is ample precedent that China's adherence to international trade deals has not been trustworthy, from recent harsh restrictions placed on Australian coal when it began capturing a bigger share of China's market, to devastating restrictions placed on South Korea's Lotte Corp.'s operations in China after South Korea allowed the United States to install an anti-missile defence system, over Beijing's protests. Then there's China's threats to effectively ban Canada's significant sales of canola seeds, which certainly hasn't stopped us from transferring high-tech applications to the Chinese military.

Once producers become dependent on the Chinese market, an asymmetrical power dynamic comes into play. The demonstrated fact is that China simply does not deal in good faith, and there is no basis for confidence that China will comply with the norms of international commerce.

Contrast this with the lack of political concessions that Canada has had to make as a consequence of our economic dependence on the U.S. (which has not used its economic power to coerce Canada into accepting missile-defence systems on Canadian soil), or forcing Canada's participation in U.S. military actions abroad. Washington has not compelled us to sell Canadian water to the parched Midwest and California, or used economic menace to induce Canada to let U.S. multinationals start mining in environmentally sensitive areas of the Canadian North.

China has zero qualms about fully leveraging economic dependence to serve its geopolitical goals throughout the world, including Canada.

Mr. Trudeau would represent Canada best if he gave China a frank review of the reasons why we cannot commit to free trade with a non-transparent, state-directed, duplicitous and corrupt economic regime. He should also brief his Chinese hosts on Canada's "Justice for Victims of Corrupt Foreign Officials Act (Magnitsky Law)" that came into effect in October.

Recently, 19 Venezuelan officials joined the list of Russians and South Sudanese on the Canadian Magnitsky sanctions list because, as the government explains, they are "responsible for, or complicit in, gross violations of internationally recognized human rights, have committed acts of significant corruption or both." Presumably the same criteria applied to Russia and Venezuela will shortly be applied to larger numbers of Chinese officials.

Or does China free trade trounce that, too?

This piece closes the loop on Justin Trudeau's naive and doomed trip to China to exact a trade deal and lip service about respecting human rights.

Canada-China relations are now ripe for a rethink

OTTAWA CITIZEN, 12 DECEMBER 2017

BESIDES SKEWERING PRIME MINISTER JUSTIN TRUDEAU'S China strategy, Beijing's gruff refusal last week to factor labour, gender or environmental rights into free trade talks likely marks Canada's last gasp in a futile, decades-long effort to engage China in global institutions on Western terms.

In the early 1980s, after "Red China" abandoned its Maoist revolutionary agenda to pursue strength and prosperity through international trade, Canada began transferring hundreds of millions of taxpayer dollars to China's post-Mao regime through the Canadian International Development Agency, the World Bank and other United Nations' agencies.

Basically, China would name a request and Canada signed a cheque. We paid for feasibility studies for the Three Gorges Dam, we sold China CANDU nuclear reactors on highly favourable terms, we funded projects to improve the quality of Chinese wheat and pork production.

Most importantly, we paid for Chinese scientists, engineers and technicians to come to Canada to acquire Canadian advanced technologies.

These programs were always characterized as "exchanges," but the money was all Canadian, with nothing given back beyond duck dinners and Great Wall tourism.

Aside from the moral missionary nature of it all, prime ministers from Jean Chrétien claimed this goodwill would eventually lead to China's democratization and implementation of rule of law. And when that happened, Canada would engage in highly productive fair trade in a huge new market, building our prosperity on China's rise. To this end, Chrétien led his memorable "Team Canada" trade missions to China.

In hindsight, we see that any economic benefits were mostly limited to a few large Canadian companies with the sophistication to navigate complex relationships with Chinese Communist business networks. Meanwhile, back home, untold thousands of Canadian workers would lose solid union jobs to China's "opening and reform."

After the failed 1989 Tiananmen democracy movement led to massive repression, pressure grew for the federal government to emphasize "human rights, democratization and good governance" in its aid-funded China programming. CIDA's Chinese counterpart, the Ministry of Foreign Economic Relations and Trade, reluctantly accepted this as a cost of keeping Canada's technology transfer funds flowing. So, China agreed to loosely structured programs designed to turn its National People's Congress into a democratic parliament, to train judges for some future independent judiciary, to encourage citizen activism on social issues, to raise awareness of gender rights, et cetera. We began a "confidential" government-to-government human rights dialogue; China even signed the UN's International Covenant on Civil and Political Rights, promising to set the stage for a free press, democratic elections and protection of indigenous and minority rights.

It was all lip service. Politicians involved from both countries knew that these were public relations exercises intended to soothe Canadians' human rights concerns.

Last week, Ottawa's cynicism with regard to appeasing Canadians on Chinese rights and freedoms did play out again. One would have to be naïve to believe that legitimate labour, gender or environmental reforms could be incorporated into a trade deal with a Marxist-Leninist dictatorship. This is a nation where Stalin is still revered as a significant forefather of Chinese Communism under current President Xi Jinping — with whom our prime minister dined just days ago.

It seems the PMO assumed the Chinese strongman would sign a joint statement referencing labour, gender and environment rights, while Justin Trudeau flew home Chamberlain-like to celebrate his squaring the circle on the conundrum of trade versus protecting Canadian values in Canada-China relations. And by the time negotiations were complete some years hence, any labour, gender and environment clauses would have been relegated to irrelevant statements of principles with no binding effect.

But, evidently unknown to Mr. Trudeau and his advisers, Xi Jinping made it crystal clear at the October Communist Party Congress that it was his predecessors' pandering to "western bourgeois false ideologies" that had led to their "lack of drive, incompetence, disengagement from the people, inaction, and corruption."

The days of Chinese lip service to Canadian wishes have definitely come to an end, but as one era ends, a new one begins. When Canada's "progressive trade agenda" died in the Great Hall of the People last week, it opened an opportunity for a serious, non-partisan re-think of how Canada should manage our role in China's comprehensive rise to power in the years and decades ahead.

While reading through a long, rambling Chinese Communist Party announcement, Burton discovered a passage buried deep inside the document saying that China was ending its two-term limit for president. This was the moment Xi Jinping seized absolute power.

A red flag for Canada after the Putinization of Xi's dictatorship

THE GLOBE AND MAIL, 26 FEBRUARY 2018

ON MONDAY, THE XINHUA NEWS AGENCY issued a long, unprecedented statement about directions from the Chinese Communist Party Central Committee to the National People's Congress regarding revisions to China's national constitution.

The People's Congress is now required to propose these revisions at its annual meeting next month. If there was any doubt that China's national legislature is anything but a toothless rubber stamp for the secretive machinations of the Communist Politburo, there isn't any more.

Hidden well inside the turgid text, at the end of Section 14, is the removal of a phrase limiting China's president and vice-president to two terms in office. So it looks as if President Xi Jinping, 64 years old, and his proposed VP, Wang Qishan, 69, are in for life. (Expect an approving tweet from Donald Trump, who must feel ever more resentful of being buckled down by the United States' comparable constitutional restriction.)

China's term limit was enacted in 1982, following a reassessment of the later years of Chairman Mao Zedong, who was supreme leader from 1935 until his death in 1976. The overwhelming consensus in China is that he stayed in power 20 years too long, with things going horribly wrong from 1957 with the large-scale purge of "rightists." This was followed by the disastrous Great Leap Forward economic campaign, which led to more than 30 million people dying of starvation. Then came a decade of massive destruction, upheaval and political purges in the Cultural Revolution (1966-76).

But at least Mao's power was somewhat constrained by colleagues such as Zhou Enlai and Liu Shaoqi, who retained their own currency as leaders from the revolutionary wars. By comparison, Mr. Xi has no such checks or balances, having already methodically purged potential rivals such as Sun Zhengcai and Bo Xilai through anti-corruption campaigns. Mr. Xi has now assumed absolute control of the party, army and state. Only violence would dislodge him from power, some sort of extreme right-wing nationalist military coup that could bring a xenophobic expansionist regime even more hostile to Canadian interests than what we face now.

Any naive hopes for a peaceful evolution to democracy are shattered against the reality that China is now a one-man dictatorship yearning to restore the archaic political norms of China's imperial past: subjects instead of citizens, the destiny of the country instead of individual or minority and collective entitlement to protection of their rights.

Moreover, another of the constitutional revisions adds "Xi Jinping Thought on Socialism with Chinese Characteristics for a New Era" as the party's ideological guide. In other words, whatever Mr. Xi says or does has the authority of supreme law in China.

The problem for Canada is that Mr. Xi has a fervent commitment to a meta-ideology that threatens the current, fraying liberal world order.

His "Chinese dream of national restoration" demands that Canada and all Western countries become subsidiary participants in the Chinese-dominated "community of the common destiny of humankind," linked by the massive "One Belt One Road" global infrastructure program. Under a previous empire, all roads led to Rome. Under Mr. Xi, all high-speed rail lines under heaven, shipping routes (including those via the Canadian Arctic) and air transport will pass through Beijing.

China is already aggressively rallying support from pro-mainland ethnic Chinese in Canada, as well China-friendly business lobbyists and politicians, through its United Front Work Department initiatives in Canada. If the political consensus in Canada is not to comply, expect China to retaliate. Britain, Australia and New Zealand have already refused to support the One Belt One Road plan; they will certainly incur Beijing's wrath, starting with economic punishment as the stick, and promise of trade and investment benefits for compliance with China's demands as the carrot.

The constitutional amendments also include new language about "the great revival of the Chinese race." The threat to Chinese Canadians is that there is a much enhanced blood-and-belonging aspect to Mr. Xi's constitutionally endorsed rhetoric. This overarching vision sees all ethnic Chinese — regardless of citizenship or number of generations abroad, even including children adopted from China — as obligated to respond to Chinese embassy pressures to facilitate China's rise, through political support for Beijing and even treasonous espionage. Canadians with family in China are already feeling pressure to demonstrate their loyalty in this way. Canada must be doing much more to protect our citizens of ethnic Chinese origin from foreign interference.

Under Xi Jinping's now unchallengeable dictatorship, the world is becoming more and more Chinese. We should ensure this does not mean that Canada has to become less and less Canadian.

Already dealing with Donald Trump's demands to rewrite the North American Free Trade Agreement, Canada now faces potentially more damaging problems. An escalating trade war between Washington and Beijing could cripple the buying power of China — a crucial customer of Canadian food and resource exports. Interestingly, while Burton was in China in 2018, many people acknowledged the U.S. tactics were justified, that Washington's claims about unfair Chinese trade practices and illegal acquisition of U.S. technology were fully valid.

Canada caught in the crossfire of the U.S.-China trade war

THE GLOBE AND MAIL, 16 AUGUST 2018

PRIME MINISTER JUSTIN TRUDEAU'S GOVERNMENT IS working furiously to offset potentially disastrous consequences of U.S. President Donald Trump's "America First" reworking of NAFTA, but that's not even the half of our problems. Trump's trade dispute with China — a bloody war of attrition between the globe's two largest economies — could cripple the buying power of a crucial customer of Canadian food and resource exports.

Many people I spoke with this summer in China readily acknowledged that the United States' tactics are justified, because Washington's claims about China's unfair trade practices and coercive or illegal acquisition of U.S. technology are fully valid.

There is a consensus among many Chinese that President Xi Jinping and his predecessors have caused China to seriously lose face, especially now that the United States has exposed Beijing's dishonourable trade policies. This violates the core Confucian teaching that upholding honesty and openness is the mark of cultured, upright government officials.

Washington demands that China take immediate, radical action to comply with World Trade Organization commitments if it expects the United States to lift crushing tariffs on Chinese imports. No more half measures or hazy promises, as proffered to U.S. presidents so many times before. With China's economy much more dependent on trade with the United States than vice versa, Mr. Trump has the upper hand.

For Mr. Xi, who has invested much of his regime's legitimacy in his own charisma, this is bad news. During his five years of power, he has dismissed previous Communist Party leaders as weak and ineffective. Mr. Xi promises to make China great again by eliminating government corruption and waste, and unifying the country on a mission to displace the United States as the world's dominant power by 2050.

But more and more Chinese are disenchanted with Mr. Xi's policies. While some are pleased to see corrupt officials get brutal comeuppance (especially factions that rival Mr. Xi's grip on power), party officials continue to enjoy enormous privilege: luxury housing, generous pensions, free medical care in world-class hospitals and special shops where it is assured that food and medicines are not dangerous because of payoffs to government regulators or unaccountable local leaders.

Mr. Xi's concept of national common purpose and social cohesion is being implemented by strengthening the surveillance state and banning liberal democratic discourse in universities and in social media. Cultural and religious rights are fiercely suppressed and a 40-year plan to assimilate the Uyghur population has led to internment camps that incarcerate hundreds of thousands of innocents in horrendous conditions.

Moreover, state TV features endless items about Beijing-funded pipelines and ports in Pakistan and Sri Lanka; bridges and sports stadiums in South Asia, South America and Africa; railways to Russia; and massive land reclamation schemes on reefs in the South China Sea. This massive infrastructure tightens China's global influence as part and parcel of the "One Belt One Road" initiative. Earlier this year, the ratings agency Fitch reported that an incomprehensible US$900-billion worth of projects are planned or under way. Chinese people recognize these projects are more about geopolitics than economic feasibility, and there is fear that China will lose even more face if unrealistic claims of global domination wither in the face of financial reality.

What Chinese people want is a country that invests in health care and education, and a desperately needed social welfare safety net. This will help the vast majority of the population who remain poor and insecure while the political elite enjoys untold wealth (often used to acquire Canadian real estate). Chinese people, increasingly fed up with unaccountable rule by a leader for life, deserve better.

There is no small irony if the Washington's trade war brings Beijing into compliance with globally accepted practices, but regardless, both Canada and China could be in for a rough economic ride so long as Mr. Trump remains President of the United States.

More than 600 days after their bogus arrests, Spavor and Kovrig were still in Chinese jails, with Canadians clamouring for their release. This column disrobes the Trudeau government's exasperating reluctance to confront China's miserable record on human rights, trade and hostage diplomacy. Pointing out Canada's "sagging reputation as a weak link in maintaining international rules-based order", the article cites a list of measures Ottawa has refused to enact.

China threatens and intimidates people within Canada as Ottawa remains silent

TORONTO STAR, 8 SEPTEMBER 2020

NOTWITHSTANDING ITS NIMBLE HANDLING of a pandemic, Justin Trudeau's government will be vulnerable in the next election if voters don't see meaningful action instead of Canada's passive rhetoric on China's human rights, trade and hostage diplomacy.

This summer, the Commons Subcommittee on International Human Rights and the Commons Special Committee on Canada-China Relations heard harrowing testimony from witnesses who say

Chinese government agents threaten them and their families in Canada and in China.

Canadian Chinese and Canadian Uighur activists told of being threatened with rape or even death if they keep speaking out against violations committed by China against the Uighurs, or the persecution of Hong Kong residents clinging to political rights.

Witnesses pleaded for Canada to stop this intimidation campaign being co-ordinated by the Chinese Embassy in Ottawa and its consulates in Montreal, Toronto, Calgary and Vancouver. All people in Canada are entitled to the protection of the Canadian Charter of Rights and Freedoms, including Chinese Canadians or citizens of China here in Canada as students or for other purposes.

Foreign Affairs Minister François-Philippe Champagne's nonresponse to calls to protect Chinese Canadians amounts to tacit consent for Beijing to continue acting as if ethnic Chinese, Tibetans and Uighurs within Canada should still be subject to repression by China's Communist regime.

Sadly, this is consistent with Canada's nonaction on China. Regarding offering sanctuary to Hong Kong activists facing persecution due to repressive moves by Beijing, we are told that Ottawa is thinking it over. Ditto to applying Magnitsky sanctions against Chinese officials complicit in genocidal measures against Uighur people, including forced sterilization of women.

These sanctions are already applied against officials in Saudi Arabia, Venezuela and other countries engaging in human rights abuses less serious than China's. If Ottawa defers these decisions as long as they have delayed ruling on Huawei 5G, Canada's sagging reputation as a weak link in maintaining international rules-based order will be confirmed.

Magnitsky sanctions would seriously impact China's "red nobility," who park dubious assets in Canada. For them this country serves as a bolt hole in case of being on the losing end of factional struggles that characterize China's unstable nondemocracy.

This includes Meng Wanzhou, the Huawei CFO with a $5-million, six-bedroom residence plus a $13-million estate more than triple that size in one of Vancouver's toniest neighbourhoods. (Meng was carrying seven passports when detained by Canadian authorities.) People like this are not so concerned about military conflicts or decoupling from the West, as they are of Magnitsky cancellation of their visas and confiscation of their overseas money and assets.

To maintain power, Party General-Secretary Xi Jinping must be seen as protecting the interests of Communist elites. If they believe his mismanagement of relations with Canada will impact them directly, Xi has a major problem. But this point appears lost on Canadian policymakers, those same people who seem in no hurry to consider a Canadian iteration of Australia's Foreign Influence Transparency Scheme Act.

That law has led to numerous former senior Australian government people resigning from the lucrative China-related boards and consultancies. Such plums are a key tactic of China's covert and corrupt approach to cultivating influential Western "friends."

What of the *sotto voce* reservations expressed about the impact of Canada doing anything that China would not like on the fate of hostages Michael Spavor and Michael Kovrig? After more than 600 days of incarceration, Ottawa's refrain "we are working very hard" to achieve their release has worn thin. The fact is, Beijing will hold these two innocent men for as long as it benefits the furtherance of China's agenda in Canada, regardless of any impact on China's global credibility.

Currently, Beijing has got us where they want us. The tragic fallacy of Canada's silence is that the longer we remain passive in the face of China's appalling violations of international trade, diplomacy and human rights, the longer we can expect Kovrig and Spavor to remain in Chinese prison hell.

Australia incurs punishing tariffs and export bans from Beijing because the Aussies had the integrity to call for an investigation into the origins of COVID; ban Huawei from Australia's 5G network; and forbid influential Australians from accepting lucrative appointments or gifts from China. The contrast with Ottawa's appeasement to China could not be more stark.

Canada takes note as China gets tough with Australia

TORONTO STAR, 16 NOVEMBER 2020

AS THE WORLD PONDERS THE SPECTACLE of Donald Trump's desperate efforts to sabotage the legitimacy of the U.S. election, on other side of the planet, China is seizing the moment to launch a full-court press to weaken the Western alliance through economic coercion, starting with drastic measures levelled against our anglosphere ally, Australia. The implications for Canada and our relations with the Biden administration are immediate and dire.

Earlier this month, Chinese importers were abruptly told to stop importing a wide range of commodities from Australia, including barley, sugar, red wine, timber, coal, lobster, copper ore and copper concentrates. Consequently, tonnes of stinking dead rock lobsters sat on the tarmac at the Shanghai Airport and thousands of crates of Australian wine caught in customs limbo. This outrageous affront follows China's specious imposition of anti-dumping duties on Australian barley, and beef export suspensions. The South China Post reported that a ban on Australian wheat could be next.

Australia will have no choice but to reciprocate by blocking imports from China, as Beijing's actions are in gross violations of the terms of its 2001 accession to the World Trade Organization. It also opens up the way for China to curry favour with the Biden administration by offering the market for these commodities in a side trade deal with the U.S. So much for the protections of the 2014 Australia-China Free Trade Agreement that Canada has long craved to duplicate.

China's anger is fired by numerous factors, including Australia's call for an international inquiry into the origins of the coronavirus, and Australia's ban of Chinese telecom giant Huawei from its 5G network due to national security concerns. But Beijing is especially furious over legislation to address China's covert, corrupt and coercive political operations to influence Australian politicians with, as a recent report by the U.K.'s Royal United Services Institute (RUSI) notes, "life-changing amounts of money."

The Chinese Communist Party newspaper *China Daily* has threatened that Australia will "suffer further pain" for fuelling anti-China sentiment by sanctioning Chinese companies, sending warships to China's doorsteps in the South China Sea and "colluding" with Washington, concluding that "Australia will pay tremendously for its misjudgment."

Chinese Foreign Ministry spokesman Wang Wenbin recently said, "We want to urge some people in Australia to earnestly reflect on its own misdeeds, do more to enhance mutual trust . . . and create the good conditions and atmosphere for practical co-operation between the two countries."

Chinese diplomats in Australia have issued statements suggesting that, to set things right, Australia should sign up to Beijing's $1.5 trillion Belt and Road infrastructure initiative and begin a "new direction of co-operation." One could imagine a future with Chinese military bases at the Port of Darwin and elsewhere along the Australian coast.

China of course wants Canada to interpret all this as an affirmation of the appeasement policy that Ottawa continues to adopt in the face of horrendous hostage diplomacy and of Beijing's arbitrary termination of Canadian agricultural import contracts that we have seen over the past two years.

Those who have urged that we treat the panda kindly, lest he show his claws and draw blood with his fangs, will urge that Canada continue ignoring the strong recommendations of Commons committees to support endangered Hong Kong democracy activists or to sanction Chinese officials complicit in the Uighur genocide. That perspective implies it would be best that Canada simply risk our alliance with the U.S. by releasing Meng Wanzhou, approving Huawei 5G and continue to allow PRC acquisition of Canadian dual-use technologies.

While Australia has strongly supported Canada over Kovrig and Spavor, it is unlikely that Ottawa will dare to stand with Australia in the face of Chinese bullying, beyond our usual carefully worded "expression of concern." But Australia's relations with China today are almost certainly Canada's tomorrow. As the RUSI report notes, citing the ex-Australian PM and China scholar Kevin Rudd, "the Chinese Communist Party despises and takes advantage of weakness, while it respects strength."

Is Canada better off giving into Chinese disdain, or should we do the right thing and stand up to China's bullying violations of the norms of international diplomacy and trade?

It is high time our government gave Canadians a clear and unambiguous answer.

Important context on why Canada needs a foreign agent registry as a matter of national security, and the government's never-explained reasons for actively resisting the pursuit of such a measure to protect our sovereignty. It's a frustrating dance that continues to go on in Ottawa

Canada needs a foreign agent registry to help it tackle China's influence

OTTAWA CITIZEN, 6 MARCH 2021

RECENTLY, ROBERT OLIPHANT, PARLIAMENTARY secretary to the foreign affairs minister, told the House of Commons that Canada is considering creating a registry of foreign agents, along the lines of Australia's Foreign Influence Transparency Scheme Act and the U.S. Foreign Agents Registration Act.

It seems like a no-brainer to expect transparency whenever someone takes a foreign state's money in expectation that they will commensurately serve the interest of the funder. But please excuse any skepticism that Canada will, any time soon, legislate a registry for former politicians, civil servants, scholars and other opinion influencers who receive such benefits from China.

Beijing incentivizes these people with lucrative board memberships and other associations with the Chinese party-state, as unregistered lobbyists to put in a quiet word with their former government colleagues. The message: Canadian companies will lose out on lucrative contracts if our federal government implements policies inflicting anything more than verbal condemnation on China's human rights violations, espionage, acquisition of key Canadian natural resources and infrastructure, and flouting of the international rules-based order in diplomacy and trade by hostage-taking and economic coercion.

These influencers represent China as proxies in public statements in Canadian newspapers and through reports from think-tanks that have accepted PRC-associated funding. They attempt to dampen Canadians' outrage over China's state behaviour, or over authorizing Huawei 5G despite stark warnings from Canadian and international security experts. They urge that we accept the myth of China's inevitable global supremacy in the wake America's decline, that Canada should compromise our commitment to our security, sovereignty and Canadian values of fairness, justice and reciprocity in relations between nations, lest we become bystanders to the "greatest changes in global history."

Even though opinion polls indicate nearly nine in 10 Canadians want our government to be much more "proactive" in relations with China, the prime minister and cabinet are apparently listening to other voices, who may be rewarded by the PRC régime, saying we should be "sophisticated and mature" in our relations with China, abiding by China's urging that we "set aside differences and seek common ground."

In the recent House of Commons resolution recognizing China's suppression of Turkic Muslims as a violation of the UN Genocide Convention, MPs across party lines voted 226-0 to pass the motion, but the prime minister instructed his cabinet to abstain, with no clear reason given. The message to Beijing is that the Trudeau government will ignore the horror taking place in China's Uyghur region, showing contempt for Canada's parliamentary democracy but pleasing the Chinese Embassy.

China's manipulation activities go far beyond rewarding Canadian influencers. Politicians, the RCMP and CSIS all acknowledge that for years Chinese agents have harassed and coerced people of Chinese origin within Canada, including Canadian Uyghurs, Tibetans, Hong Kongers, PRC students and dissidents. But none of the large cohort of Chinese agents in Canada has been made accountable by being charged in court, or, if they are Chinese diplomats, by being declared persona non grata and sent packing.

There is also alarming evidence that Canadian dual-use military technologies and other classified data are being illegally transferred to China's party-state-military-security-industrial complex, by Canadian and Chinese researchers and spies. Not a single person has been arrested and charged in Canada, in part because co-opted pro-China voices in Ottawa counsel that we not offend the PRC by arresting any of their spies.

This latest statement by MP Oliphant, that the government is "actively considering" creating a registry of foreign agents, follows a familiar pattern. To appease or distract public opinion, the Trudeau government dangles a series of hollow promises, then just kicks the can down the road.

Canadians should demand that their government stop with the lip service and follow through with this now. As the old Lerner and Loewe show tune puts it "Sing me no song, read me no rhyme, please don't explain. Show me!"

After the University of Alberta refused to share information about a major donation it received from a Chinese Communist Party-linked billionaire in Hong Kong, this piece explains how Canadian researchers' partnerships with Chinese academics are different from collaborations with scholars from other countries

In Canadian universities, China's espionage is hiding in plain sight

EDMONTON JOURNAL, 17 MAY 2021

CANADA'S FREE SOCIETY IS BASED ON cultural expectations of reciprocal fairness and goodwill in our dealings with fellow citizens. This is what makes Canada a great place to live, and so attractive to immigrants. But our trusting nature is also vulnerable to being exploited by foreign actors with agendas that threaten our security and sovereignty.

Consider China, whose intricate manipulation practices have had enormous success in transferring research data from Canadian universities in strategically sensitive areas that serve Beijing's purposes. According to former CSIS director Richard Fadden, these areas include avionics, space technology, nuclear science and high-level optics research.

The fact is, China's interference and espionage activities are hiding in plain sight in our open institutions. We need transparency about what these activities comprise, which Canadians are receiving benefits from agents of foreign states, and what form these benefits take.

Recent and troubling media reports reveal that, in 2018, the China Institute at the University of Alberta accepted a major donation from Hong Kong-based billionaire Jonathan Koon-Shum Choi, but refuses to disclose the size of Mr. Choi's gift, the purposes to which the money has been allocated, and who are the de facto beneficiaries of this largesse.

Choi is a member of the Standing Committee of the Chinese People's Political Consultative Conference (CPPCC), part of the Chinese Communist Party's United Front Work Department (UFWD), whose main mission is to gain outside support for Beijing's political agenda.

As the U of A is a public institution, surely Alberta taxpayers deserve transparency regarding any money that supports or influences the university's research.

Under an agreement with China's Minister of Science and Technology, U of A researchers have had access to at least 50 state labs in China since 2005, while upward of 60 professors have received funding for more than 90 joint projects with state and national labs in China. Likewise, at the University of British Columbia, more than 300 professors have significant professional interest in China, and faculty have partnerships with over 100 Chinese institutions.

But agreements through China's Ministry of Science and Technology are not like those with partners in democratic societies. These are not simply benign, mutually beneficial collaborations between autonomous scholars seeking to expand the frontiers of science and human understanding, as much as the UFWD would have us believe.

In China, professors are cadre-ranked state employees, their research dictated by the state ministries to which their universities and labs are subordinate. Their ultimate goal is to advance the Chinese Communist Party's five-year plans for domestic development and global geo-strategic advantage.

China would not be funding Canadian researchers if there were no ability to access the data which the professors generate. This is about obtaining information or intellectual property that could serve the PRC's economic and military objectives. Indeed, some Canadian participants over the long term appear to derive significant Chinese income streams beyond their university salaries, through lucrative PRC-associated board appointments and commercial inducements.

The money is an effective device. Chinese grants help Canadians pursue research projects that might not have been so well funded by Canada's Natural Sciences and Engineering Research Council. The profs gain prestige from undertaking work in important and sensitive areas, enjoy wonderful hospitality in China, and benefit from considerable talented Chinese research assistance — providing they hand over their work to the Chinese state to develop. The strategy spends years cultivating a Canadian target, with the recipients often not fully aware of what they're getting themselves into.

It is reassuring that Alberta government officials have promised to protect Canada's national interest by curtailing U of A collaborations with China in strategically sensitive science and technology, but will Ottawa initiate federal legislation such as requiring transparency in reporting of foreign sources of income? There is a powerful pro-PRC lobby in Ottawa, mostly retired politicians who are on China-related boards, including Canadian companies and law firms that benefit from the PRC. In taking China's money, they are expected to support the interests of the PRC in Canada in return.

Beijing seems confident that, once Canadian public outrage fades over the latest reports of China's shameless flouting of the norms of international relations, the Canadians on the PRC gravy train will resume quietly lobbying for Ottawa's restraint in any new measures. This United Front work is a sophisticated engagement of Canada, and the PRC always seems to end up on top.

After Canada is excluded from a new security dialogue involving Australia, Japan, India and the US, this piece explores why its allies don't trust Canada to be inside the tent.

Canada looks on as Biden rallies other allies to counter China

TORONTO STAR, 21 JULY 2021

THE WHITE HOUSE HAS CONFIRMED THAT U.S. President Joe Biden plans to meet later this year with his Japanese, Australian and Indian counterparts — a four-country grouping dubbed the "Quadrilateral Security Dialogue" or QUAD.

The announcement came just days after Chinese Communist Party General-Secretary Xi Jinping marked the centenary of the party with an incendiary oratory that was short on Marxism but long on nationalist promises "to build a new type of international relations."

This is Xi's doctrine of "the community of the common destiny of mankind" under future People's Republic of China (PRC) global domination, which includes making irrelevant the current institutions that promote peace, prosperity and justice, such as the United Nations, World Trade Organization, G-20 and G-7.

The latter's get-together earlier this summer in Cornwall, England was dismissed by China's U.K. embassy, saying "the days when global decisions were dictated by a small group of countries are long gone."

Xi himself made clear China "will not accept sanctimonious preaching from those who feel they have the right to lecture us," and such opponents of the PRC's policies of genocide and hostage diplomacy will "have their heads bashed bloody." The latter colourful phrase was edited out of the official English-language translation of the speech, but was enthusiastically cited in jingoist Chinese social media.

There is an urgent need for Ottawa to fund programs that train young Canadians in contemporary Communist China studies, including Mandarin language studies. Chinese propagandists blatantly distort official statements through shameless mistranslation and subtle edits for foreign audiences.

The PRC's engagement of Canada employs agents fluent in English or French, so how can we expect to accurately comprehend the situation when our people mostly can barely read or understand Chinese and rely largely on translations provided by Chinese authorities?

Since the 2018 arrest of Huawei CFO Meng Wanzhou and China's retaliatory detention of Michael Kovrig and Michael Spavor — combined with Beijing's coercive cancellation of Canadian agricultural contracts, and revelations of China's program of genocide against Uyghur Muslims — Canadian public support has plunged below 20 per cent for Ottawa's strategy of quiet diplomacy and a lack of resetting its China policy.

However, the need to counter "anti-Asian hate" in Canada is being misconstrued by Canadian commentators with agendas, people who argue against Canadians raising such concerns as Beijing's reluctance to disclose data for an international investigation of the origins of COVID-19, or demanding China give the UN Human Rights High Commissioner unconditional access to travel in Uyghur regions to get the truth about their situation.

Some of these pundits promote an appalling implication that Chinese Canadians are somehow connected with the malign policies of the Chinese Communist Party.

So while Biden demands that Western powers need to act now to counter a resurgent China, he evidently does not have Canada with him. Canada's hesitancy in confronting the PRC is partly assisted by influential people in Ottawa who enjoy lucrative board memberships, or associations with law firms, or well-connected Canadian businesses that have close ties with PRC state business.

China has established an environment where Canadian policymakers are subject to promises of personal benefit in return for not inhibiting PRC interests in Canada. Canadians are right to demand transparency on the nature of such ties to a hostile foreign power, and full disclosure of financial or other rewards thus generated.

Unfortunately, as Canadians anticipate a fall election, Conservative MP Kenny Chiu's private member's Bill C-282 — "An Act to establish the Foreign Influence Registry," described by him as intended "to recognize and increase vigilance to shine a light on harmful interference from abroad" — will likely not get any further than its first reading back in April.

Our government's increasingly pointed rhetoric with no substantive followup only confirms the weakness of Canada's position with China, while Ottawa's attempts at clever diplomacy in trying to steer a middle path between the PRC and the U.S. has only debased Washington's faith in Canada's commitment to the integrity of the international rules-based order.

Prime Minister Justin Trudeau needs to phone President Biden to assure him of Canada's support for positive determinations that come out of the QUAD meeting. Then we should not just talk the talk but stand up and show some courage of our convictions.

This ominous essay about how autocrats like Putin, and especially Xi, aim to supplant the world's liberal democracies seems even more prescient in the second term of Donald Trump's presidency. In dismembering the infrastructure and agencies that sustain American democracy, he seems bent on ushering in the end of 80 years of the post-war Western alliance.

Time to wake up and take megalomaniacs seriously

TORONTO STAR, 2 MARCH 2022

VLADIMIR PUTIN'S MEANDERING RANT ON THE eve of invading Ukraine demonstrated that his deranged torment and bitterness over failing to restore Russia's imperial greatness has advanced to psychopathological megalomania.

In his 70th year and with more than two decades in power, Putin is obsessed with achieving military dominance beyond Ukraine to the other nations of the defunct Warsaw Pact, at any cost. Convinced he has been foiled by American treachery, he will not be deterred by massive sanctions that bring great suffering to ordinary Russians. Putin threatens to deploy nuclear weapons if he doesn't get his way. If we did not take his menacing speeches seriously before, we had better do so now.

China is another nuclear power that could threaten that option to achieve its international ambitions. Chinese leader Xi Jinping, who is also approaching a third term that will take him to his early 70s, will be closely watching Putin's attempt to vanquish Ukrainian nationalism for lessons on how to subjugate Taiwan. But Xi's speeches, similar to Putin's, look beyond Taiwan, descending into a dark, resentful rhetoric over the West's suppression of China's "national rejuvenation."

Xi is confident that, under his leadership, China's civilizational norms, as he interprets them, will displace the liberal West in a new China-dominated global order. He foresees this "community of the common destiny of mankind" being in place by 2050. Under his Belt and Road global infrastructure initiative, the world's economy will be restructured to place China definitively at the centre of power; all the belts and roads will lead to Beijing. It is a delusional overblown ambition, but if Xi sees this promised future slipping away, China could lash out at the world in the same dangerous ways as Putin is doing now.

Canada has until now given Xi's ambitions short shrift. Serious China expertise in our foreign ministry, CSIS, the RCMP, CSE and DND is thin on the ground. There has been no political will to get more Canadians fluent in Mandarin and thus more attuned to what is really going on with the Chinese Communist Party, domestically, internationally, and here in Canada.

In fact we even enable Xi's regime by submitting to Chinese embassy threats to punish Canada economically through trade sanctions if we respond in any substantive way to China's robust industrial espionage operations in Canada, or coercion of ethnic Chinese people in Canada to serve the interests of the Communist Party regime, or China's very sophisticated influence operations targeting Canadians with influence on Canada's foreign policy formulation.

What we need to do immediately is stop pussyfooting around on Huawei 5G and make a clear statement, to China and the world, that we are not duped by Beijing's assurances that Huawei is not a function of the Chinese regime and its military intelligence services.

We need to work with our allies to stand up collectively to sanction China's flouting of the international rules-based order in trade and diplomacy. It is too late for Canada to credibly take the lead in this effort, but we should join Australia in urging our European allies to set aside petty national egos that have obstructed moving beyond rhetoric on this front. It only plays into China's slick and well-resourced divide-and-conquer strategy.

Canada must also become much more urgently engaged with Third World nations who are understandably tempted to sign over their sovereignty and security in exchange for China's Belt and Road development funding.

The atrocities in Ukraine demonstrate that megalomaniac autocrats will not abide by our perceptions of the self-interest of nations over which they have inflicted dominance. Canada needs to follow Germany and significantly upgrade our military capacity to meet the increasingly uncertain geostrategic challenges of which the invasion of Ukraine is just the harbinger.

We must do all we can to support the transition to democratic regimes in Russia and China so they can become responsible members in the community of nations.

COVID's hangover lingered and China's economy was reeling. Xi Jinping was suddenly vulnerable as he sought to reassure a population suffering under his Stalinist policies that squeezed living standards and fuelled China's legendary corruption. After years of cementing his own power and eliminating political rivals, Xi's track record was now his biggest liability.

China's growing economic angst is another political threat for Xi

THE GLOBE AND MAIL, 28 AUGUST 2023

AS CHINA'S ECONOMY TANKS IN DRAMATIC fashion, there are growing signs that the regime is scrambling to avoid any civil unrest fanned by the downturn.

Earlier this month, after seven consecutive months of rising youth unemployment, Beijing announced it will stop releasing jobless statistics for young people. Official figures put unemployment among 16- to 24-year-olds in urban areas at 21.3 per cent; objective observers suspect it is much higher than that.

But leaders are concerned by more than the spectre of frustrated urban youth staging public demonstrations against the Chinese Communist Party. Another time bomb is the disintegration of China's housing and real estate sector in medium and small cities, where a growing number of people have prepaid for apartments that may never get built.

Developments like these, combined with a steep drop in foreign investment, are diminishing Xi Jinping's charisma as China's wisest steward (as per his own philosophical essay, Thought on Socialism with Chinese Characteristics for a New Era). It seems his Stalinist bent for economic policies — favouring state control over private enterprise, underhanded bad-faith dealings in international trade, and economic coercion — isn't working as expected. China seemed stunned this year when the U.S. responded to Mr. Xi's new economic gospel by imposing tariffs on a wide range of Chinese imports, and cracking down on China's covert acquisition of U.S. technologies with military applications.

More significantly, the end of the economic boom threatens China's "post-Tiananmen bargain" in which citizens tolerate marginalized civic freedoms and rule of law in return for continuously improving living standards. Suddenly, Mr. Xi seems politically vulnerable. His rule has been markedly more repressive than those of his recent predecessors — reversing Deng Xiaoping's 1980s initiatives of "opening and reform" and exhortations to "liberate thought" against Maoist dogma — and because Mr. Xi has purged all his political rivals over the past 10 years, when things go wrong in this era, the buck stops with him.

Mr. Xi's rap sheet includes the COVID-19 fiasco, wherein Communist officials, desperate to protect themselves from public scorn, lied about the cause and human-to-human transmission of the virus, thereby endangering the health of ordinary citizens. This was followed by Beijing's abrupt reversal of its draconian "zero-COVID" quarantine policies, leading to massive outbreaks of illness and death.

Everybody in China knows that the Party's statistics about COVID deaths, and its propaganda about the 180-degree policy shift, were false; the day-to-day reality confronting people all across the country bore no resemblance to what was being reported by state media. Mr. Xi lied to the people. The people know he lied to them.

The impression of Xi Jinping being firmly in command of the Communist Party is also being blurred by signs of discontent within China's military leadership. This month, it emerged that Mr. Xi dismissed two generals commanding China's Rocket Force nuclear arsenal, Li Yuchao and Xu Zhongbo; neither has been seen since. Mr. Li's deputy Liu Guangbin has also disappeared, along with former deputy Zhang Zhenzhong. And Wu Guohua, deputy commander of the Rocket Force, reportedly committed suicide in July.

Several weeks ago, foreign minister and influential policy maker Qin Gang suddenly disappeared and was removed from his post without explanation. Speculation has been furious. As a barometer of China's stability, veteran China-watchers say that in this environment, any sudden changes of senior officials are seen as signs of weakness, instability or opposition to Mr. Xi's regime by Communist insiders.

If Mr. Xi has indeed compromised in his ability to weather political damage because of his handling of the economy, his mishandling of COVID, or sudden disappearances of his senior officials, then these will only add to longer-term grievances that have quietly accumulated during his rule: the persecution of #MeToo protesters, China's growing income gap, the economic privileging of "red nobility" elites, the unfair and corrupt legal system, pervasive state surveillance and strict censorship of social media.

Against this backdrop, unemployed youth who feel resentful and badly done by could, as Chairman Mao put it in quite a different context, be the spark that sets off the prairie fire. There is much precedent for this in Chinese history.

After years of ignoring demands to confront foreign interference with Canada's sovereignty and democracy, the federal government abruptly announces it will introduce Bill C-70 (An Act respecting countering foreign interference) in response to the initial report of Justice Marie-Josée Hogue's inquiry into foreign interference. It was nice to be able to write a column that was optimistic about a Canadian government approach to China.

At last, Canada is confronting the problem of foreign influence

THE GLOBE AND MAIL, 14 MAY 2024

LAST WEEK, MINISTER OF PUBLIC SAFETY and Democratic Institutions Dominic LeBlanc announced that the federal government would introduce Bill C-70 (An Act respecting countering foreign interference) in response to the initial report of Justice Marie-Josée Hogue's public inquiry into foreign interference. That was a surprise — both the announcement itself, and how well the bill was drafted.

In recent years, many China watchers have developed a layer of cynicism, or at least low expectations, regarding Ottawa's pronouncements on China. For nearly a decade, many Canadians — myself included —

have been calling for strong legislation and upgraded safeguards in the name of protecting Canada against foreign interference threats.

Even this spring's testimony at the Hogue Inquiry, which prompted public demands for full transparency from anyone who influences Canada's China policy — specifically, around whether or not they have a conflict of interest because they receive money or other benefits from Beijing — left many observers resigned to yet more rounds of "it's complicated" from the Prime Minister and his cabinet.

Now, Ottawa has proposed a tough bill that would "deter foreign principals from making efforts to influence political or governmental processes in Canada in a non-transparent manner," including by introducing the Foreign Influence Transparency and Accountability Act (FITAA), which creates a foreign-influencer registry.

What led to the sudden shift is murky. But it looks like this legislation will be passed mostly unamended through Parliament, regardless of which party wins the next election. Once you factor in normal timelines for reviewing and refining proposed legislation, and allow for an election in the next year, the Act could be implemented by 2027.

Concerns previously raised by some senior Liberals — that it will be comparable in its effects to the 1923 Chinese Exclusion Act or the internment of Japanese Canadians in the Second World War, or that it will fuel anti-Asian racism in Canada — have suddenly vaporized. (That speculation had always lacked evidence, anyway.)

It is apparent that much of the new legislation is patterned on Australia's 2018 Foreign Influence Transparency Scheme Act. In the run-up to that law being enacted, several prominent Australian political figures resigned from China-related boards and consultancies, including Andrew Robb, who, as minister for trade and investment from 2013 to 2016, had been responsible for shaping the China-Australia Free Trade Agreement.

Months after stepping down from cabinet, Mr. Robb announced that he had become a "high-level consultant" for the Landbridge Group, a Chinese company that in 2015 had been granted a 99-year lease on Port Darwin in northern Australia; that role paid him nearly $800,000 a year. In 2019, just before Australia launched its foreign-influencer registry, it emerged that Mr. Robb had quietly resigned from his consultancy. Here in Canada, as our own new legislation nears implementation, we can expect similar resignations by prominent figures from Chinese boards and consultancies.

While FITAA won't be in effect for some time, its abrupt promulgation should have a more immediate dampening effect on the operations of Beijing's agents. Elite Canadians will suddenly realize that accepting lucrative positions on Chinese boards and consultancies will be seen as nothing more than a humiliating moral compromise: agreeing to the compensation, free trips to Beijing and business opportunities will require quietly supporting any CCP foreign-policy outrage Xi Jinping that comes up with, and being complicit in genocide in Xinjiang and other violations of international human rights law going on inside China.

One wonders if, in her final report in December, Justice Hogue will provide damning insights into potential Chinese coercion of high-level Canadian government officials. The more revelations that come to the fore through the declassification of CSIS assessments, the more Canadians will wonder how high the rot goes.

Emily Brontë once described May as "the month of expectation, the month of wishes, the month of hope." Hopefully, Justice Hogue's promising initial report and Bill C-70 released this month will mark the opening of a new and sunnier era in Canada-China relations.

This article observes how China spends years cultivating people who it hopes will someday be positioned to influence Canada's policy makers. Most Canadians would be oblivious to, and stunned by, this interference targeting their government, perhaps their own MP.

Here's how China turns our politicians into pawns (hint: they're letting it happen)

TORONTO STAR, 13 JUNE 2024

THE NATIONAL SECURITY AND INTELLIGENCE COMMITTEE of Parliamentarians' stunning allegation that federal politicians are helping foreign governments manipulate Canadian politics further inflamed the perception of our leaders standing by as Chinese agents in Canada sabotage our democratic institutions.

This is about more than foreign powers rigging election outcomes.

China's Ministry of State Security (MSS) has a two-pronged strategy for turning western legislators into Beijing's proxies.

The first tactic is *huaren canzheng*: getting persons of Chinese origin elected to public office, at all levels. Allegations of China's consulate in Toronto busing in young Chinese nationals to stuff a Liberal nomination meeting and providing false IDs to indicate these youngsters were residents in the riding, is classic MSS playbook for swaying elections in countries with lax democratic processes.

Beijing expects anyone of Chinese origin, as descendants of the mythical Yellow Emperor Huangdi, has an irrevocable requirement of loyalty to China.

The second is long-term cultivation of people who are not ethnic Chinese but who can influence Canada's policies to promote Chinese interests. It typically starts early in a politician's career, "spreading the net wide" to support specific candidates, often through false-front organizations. Those who wittingly or "semi-wittingly" become China's proxies will often be given free trips to China through "friendship associations", including the Canada-China Legislative Association.

Beijing will have won the lottery if any of the parliamentarians cited in the latest NSICOP report has risen to federal Cabinet, with access to Cabinet secrets.

Subverting Canadian officials can involve bribery, blackmail — or "honey pots." Fifteen years ago, MP Bob Dechert, Parliamentary secretary to Foreign Minister John Baird, admitted exchanging flirtatious e-mails with Shi Rong, a young Xinhua news agency "reporter" based in Canada. When it emerged that she had never published an article in the Chinese press, Shi disappeared to China, resurfacing later as a scholar at Harvard's Kennedy School of Government, where many future U.S. politicians spend their salad years.

Being a "friend" to China while in a position of influence can bring reward years later, when the politician or civil servant quietly returns to the private sector.

Beijing approaches subversion as a marathon, not a sprint. When former Australian prime minister Bob Hawke travelled to China after leaving office, then-president Jiang Zemin greeted him with the words, "China never forgets its friends, and we want you to know we regard you as one of our best friends."

In the 1980s, as PM, Hawke had implored Australia's South Pacific neighbours to embrace China as a pillar of regional politics. After leaving politics, Hawke accepted several directorships and consultancies relating to China, which brought considerable income.

In Canada it will be difficult for our future "Foreign Influence Transparency and Accountability Act" to track the silent path of payoffs for officials who took the bait years earlier. There are indications that not a few former cabinet ministers and foreign ministry officials, who in retirement have lucrative associations with China, may have been at least "semi-witting" beneficiaries of China's corrupt operations.

CSIS and the RCMP will be challenged in tackling the subversion of federal and provincial parliamentarians. Powerful office holders would obviously resist acknowledging that they had been played years earlier by Chinese security agents, gradually slipping into a velvet trap of disloyalty to Canada.

At the highest levels of government, officials admitting they let this activity expand on their watch would diminish their legacy and their public-facing partisan inclinations. So they keep quiet and China is never made to account for egregious violations of diplomatic relations.

To MPs inclined to continue cultivating friendly relations with Chinese regime agents: be aware that implied promises of future rewards for advancing Beijing's interests often vanish once a politician leaves office and is no longer useful. A lot of former MPs have been ghosted by their Chinese friends when they seek the anticipated rewards.

Retirement life on the generous Parliamentary pension scheme is a just reward for loyal service to Canada. Just say no to the Chinese money.

HOSTAGE DIPLOMACY

Four years before China jailed the Two Michaels on bogus charges, Canadian missionaries Kevin and Julia Garrett were arrested in the cafe they'd operated in a backwater Chinese city and, ridiculously, charged with conducting military espionage. As with Michaels Kovrig and Spavor, the Garretts' arrest was Beijing's retaliation after Prime Minister Stephen Harper accused China of hacking into computers at Canada's National Research Council, and after Canada sent alleged Chinese agent Su Bin to the U.S. to face serious charges of stealing aerospace technologies.

Canadians detained in China are pawns in a bigger geopolitical game

THE GLOBE AND MAIL, 7 AUGUST 2014

VANCOUVER NATIVES KEVIN AND JULIA DAWN Garratt, currently being held in Dandong, China, on suspicion of military espionage, were visited in prison by a Canadian consular official earlier this week. Reports are that both remain well, but are "very frustrated and confused."

Well they might be. They are the proprietors of Peter's Coffee House where, with contemporary Christian music playing in the background, patrons can indulge in a burger and apple pie all the while enjoying the view out the front window of the cruise boats on the Yalu River, and in the far distance on the opposite shore, North Korean border guards with their AK-47 assault rifles at the ready.

According to reports, Kevin Garratt told the congregation of the Terra Nova church in Surrey, B.C., last November that God told the couple to go to Dandong and open a coffee house. "We serve the best coffee on the border . . . and we do some other things too," he said. "We're trying to reach North Korea with God, with Jesus and practical assistance."

Their arrest therefore might not be entirely unexpected. They held illegal Sunday worship services at their restaurant and were active in assisting North Korean Christians who cross the border illegally to trade in China. And they were active in sending desperately needed grain and cooking oil to underground Christian communities on the other side. Thus they would be ripe targets for the Chinese government's current campaign against the rapidly growing Christian church in China.

So how is it that the Chinese ministry of foreign affairs news release makes no mention of the Garratts' religious work but instead indicates that Kevin and Julia Dawn Garratt are "suspected of collecting and stealing intelligence material in Dandong about Chinese military targets and important national defense research projects, and engaging in activities threatening to Chinese national security"?

The key to understanding this appears to be the reference in the Chinese charge to their alleged gathering of intelligence about "important national defense research projects." The parallel to Prime Minister Stephen Harper's very explicit condemnation of China for the cyber-hacking of computers at the National Research Council last week is none too subtle. China's security agencies are not known for their subtlety.

Foreign Minister John Baird's direct and forceful follow-up with the government of China about this — he happened to be in Beijing at the time the hacking of the NRC computers came to light — probably exacerbated China's annoyance at Mr. Harper's public outing of entities of the government for their cyber-theft of "important national defense research projects" that the NRC was engaged in relating to aerospace technology.

The claim that Kevin and Julia Dawn Garratt would somehow or other be able to gain access to the hard drives of Chinese defense research establishment computers is hardly credible. This is the stuff of James Bond movies, not real life Christian evangelists in a backwater like Dandong. It really would be a Mission Impossible for the Garratts.

But the fact that the charges are so blatantly false is part of the taunting message to our Prime Minister. While it was the normal thing for foreign nationals arrested in China in the 50s and 60s to be accused of being spies for hostile powers, we have not seen this sort of thing since the end of the Mao-era Cultural Revolution. But under the neo-Leninist political rule of Xi Jinping, these are strange and retro political times in China at present.

Nevertheless, the Chinese security agencies may have underestimated the political sensitivities of this matter in Canada. Two committed Christians involved in aid work to North Korea will have a very strong support constituency within Mr. Harper's cabinet and the Conservative Party base. If the Garratts are subject to the usual Chinese police interrogation techniques and end up forced to make a false confession on television, or, worse, they are sentenced to death or a life sentence in the Chinese gulag, this matter will have a long term chilling effect on Canada-China relations.

Hopefully the Chinese authorities will see their way clear to deport Mr. and Mrs. Garratt back to Canada before Mr. Harper makes his next China tour scheduled for November.

These good people are the innocent victims of a geopolitical game that they should have no part in.

Shortly before their arrest in 2014, Burton visited Kevin and Julia Garratt's cafe in Dandong, a Chinese city on the border with North Korea. Two years later, with their release finally secured, this article discusses what led to their detention on ridiculous charges, as well as the complex interaction between China and Canada and the public outrage in Canada.

Garratt's release a win for Canada – and China

THE GLOBE AND MAIL, 17 SEPTEMBER 2016

THE PHOTOGRAPHS RELEASED BY HIS FAMILY show Kevin Garratt at the Vancouver Airport looking a little thinner but with good colour, and very happy to be home. That being said, one cannot expect that more than two years' incarceration in a Chinese prison has not seriously affected his health and wellbeing. The tragedy of it all is that Mr. Garratt was the innocent victim of a trivial geopolitical game played out with appalling disregard for his human rights by the government of China.

Before their arrests, Mr. Garratt and his wife Julia had been in China discreetly proclaiming the Gospel of Jesus for more than 30 years, most recently serving coffee and pie at their cafe in Dandong. By coincidence, I was there just before its closure. The mood music was

Christian contemporary. From the table by the window one could just make out the North Korean border guards carrying AK47s on the far side of the Yalu River.

In 2014, there was a campaign in China, presumably at the behest of North Korea, to clear foreign Christian missionaries out of towns on the Chinese side of the China-Korea border. Most of them had been working with North Korean Christians to relieve the severe deprivation among the poor living in the border area. On this basis, it's likely that Mr. Garratt was identified by Chinese authorities as a candidate for deportation back to Canada.

Around this time, then-prime minister Stephen Harper made a statement condemning agents of China for hacking into National Research Council computers holding secret Canadian aerospace research data. Mr. Harper's statement was strongly condemned by the Chinese government as "irresponsible." Not long after, the Chinese State Security Ministry, already with the Garratts in its sights, and in a petulant and ill-conceived tit-for-tat, arrested Mr. and Mrs. Garratt on the basis they had being purloining Chinese state defense research secrets.

The accusation was tragically absurd. Mr. Garratt was then subject to harsh regime of interrogation, with a view to getting him to falsely confess that he was a spy for Canada. In a tribute to Mr. Garratt's personal fortitude, he evidently was not prepared to sign off on whatever incriminating fiction the Chinese authorities cooked up, so he remained incarcerated.

Shortly thereafter, the Chinese government proposed sending the Garratts home if Ottawa agreed to repatriate Chinese national Su Bin to Beijing instead of sending him to the United States to face serious espionage charges. This would have let Beijing save face by ridding themselves of the problem of being unable to provide any credible explanation for why Mr. Garratt had been arrested and held for so long without due process of law. But ultimately Mr. Su preferred to do a plea bargain with the Americans, pleading guilty to all charges, causing the Chinese regime more embarrassment.

It is clear that the Chinese government underestimated the degree of Canadian public outrage over Canadian citizens unjustly imprisoned in foreign lands for ill-defined political reasons. When Chinese Foreign Minister Wang Yi was in Canada last June he insisted on a meeting with Prime Minister Justin Trudeau, a move that went beyond normal diplomatic protocol. At that 15 minute confab, Mr. Trudeau — rather than showing ritual deference to a senior representative of the Middle Kingdom — instead used the occasion to explain to Mr. Wang at length that Mr. Garratt's continued imprisonment was severely constraining the possibilities for greater engagement, which China was expecting from the new Liberal government. One can understand why, when Mr. Garrett's name was brought up at a press conference shortly thereafter, Mr. Wang lost his composure and delivered the diatribe that has marked him forever as a diplomatic philistine.

Mr. Garratt's return to Canada occurred unexpectedly at the mid-point between Mr. Trudeau's return from his lengthy China visit and Chinese Premier Li Keqiang's trip to Canada next week. Had Mr. Garratt still been in prison it would have been very difficult for Mr. Li to argue convincingly that Canada should be repatriating corrupt Chinese officials, or indeed negotiating a formal extradition treaty with China. Now the implication is that Canada has a reciprocal obligation to give China something back.

For Mr. Trudeau, this is a significant win as well. It demonstrates that his policy of a full-court-press engagement with Chinese authorities is not counter to Canadian human rights concerns. Mr. Trudeau was able to get Mr. Garratt back where Mr. Harper and his policies of conditional engagement failed. It does open the way for Mr. Trudeau to respond to China with the pipeline to B.C. that it wants so badly, and takes the pressure off accusations that he is compromising Canadian interests by encouraging Chinese state investment in Canada.

The Garratts are fundamentally good people who by all accounts are universally liked and admired by all who know them. All Canadians celebrate Mr. Garratt's release.

As diplomatic crises go, this was incendiary. After Meng Wanzhou's arrest in Vancouver, China jailed Michaels Spavor and Kovrig in revenge. Canadians were outraged. Incensed Beijing officials wondered why Canada's politicians didn't simply overrule police and send Meng home. This essay examines political and cultural forces behind the historic collapse in Canada-China relations and in public opinion toward China, leaving a wound that will not heal for generations.

A thorny path lies ahead for Canadian-Chinese relations

THE GLOBE AND MAIL, 31 JANUARY 2019

THERE IS NO TURNING BACK THIS clock.

The Chinese government's ugly response to the arrest of Huawei chief financial officer Meng Wanzhou — both the arbitrary "hostage diplomacy" arrests of Canadians Michael Kovrig and Michael Spavor, and the "death threat diplomacy" of resentencing alleged drug smuggler Robert Schellenberg from prison to execution — has led to revulsion and repugnance across Canada.

China and Canada now have to come to terms with the fact that — even after Ms. Meng leaves the comfort of her Vancouver mansion to either face U.S. justice or fly back to Beijing unextradited, and Mr.

Kovrig and Mr. Spavor are freed from harsh punitive custody in secret interrogation jails — there will be no return to the diplomatic dynamic that existed before the Huawei executive's detainment. Beijing's dark retaliation will have a permanent and far reaching impact on future Canada-China relations.

In retrospect, we can see that Canada's approach to China, up until the detention of the two Canadians, had become dysfunctional. It amounted to a foreign policy designed to serve the interests of Canada's business and government elite, emphasizing, over all else, the promotion of Canadian prosperity by seeking greater access to China's burgeoning market.

Beijing dangled the prospect of vast riches to starry-eyed, greedy vested interests, but demanded major concessions in return. These included: the removal of legal barriers to Chinese state acquisition of companies in Canada's energy and resources sectors, and allowing imported Chinese workers to build the necessary infrastructure; letting China acquire Canadian technology without "discriminatory trade restrictions"; signing a functionally one-sided extradition treaty so Beijing can seize Chinese expats who had fallen afoul of the regime and fled to Canada; and, despite dire warnings from Canadian security officials and their counterparts in the Five Eyes intelligence-sharing consortium, the installation of Huawei 5G technology throughout our telecommunications networks.

Some in Ottawa did not want to scuttle a trade deal by doing anything deemed by the Chinese embassy as offensive or "hurting the feelings of the Chinese people", such as challenging the activities of their intelligence operatives in Canada. For example, when a closed-door parliamentary panel discussion last fall published its report, it noted that "panellists agreed that it was important for Canada to avoid the excesses that have characterized the Chinese interference debate in the U.S. and Australia ... The fact that Australia turned to new legislation as well as the creation of a 'National Counter Foreign Interference Coordinator' should . . . not be taken as a model to be replicated" by Canada.

So, if Ottawa was considering the appointment of such a co-ordinator, or the allocation of more, and desperately needed, resources to the China operations of the RCMP and CSIS, this parliamentary panel put that thinking to bed, as they would lead to bad consequences for people who are friendly or possibly beholden to Beijing. "The bigger issue that all parties need to keep in perspective," declared the panel, "is Canada's relationship with China, and how to build stronger political, economic and cultural ties that are mutually beneficial."

Presumably the same ethos of avoidance would apply for Canada's response for any number of issues, including the rights of interned Uyghurs, Hong Kong, Taiwan, Tibet or China's military expansion into the South China Sea which blatantly violates international law.

An article this week in China's *Global Times* revealed its government's anger at the firing of Canadian ambassador John McCallum, a decision it characterized as "political interference." The article attributes Ottawa's "stand against Beijing" to pressure from "Canada's current public opinion" instigated by "some Canadian media and reporters." Beijing wants their Canadian China-friends to get back into line, threatening that "the Trudeau government must properly deal with China-Canada relations, or it should be prepared for Beijing's further retaliation."

Further retaliation or not, a Canadian prime minister cannot order a judge to authorize the return of Ms. Meng to Beijing. Hopefully, during her upcoming extradition hearing, she will cut a plea bargain with the U.S. authorities to go to the United States voluntarily, and put an end to this nightmare for Canada.

If, as part of this deal, Ms. Meng was prepared to explain to the U.S. government exactly what the relationship is between Huawei and China's intelligence, security and military apparatus, that would certainly clarify things for all of us, including how — or if — the Canada-China relationship can be reset.

Canadian public opinion will never enable Ottawa to grant the concessions Beijing wants. The post-Meng relationship requires that Canada regain the respect of China's regime by standing up for our interests and values. In this complicated landscape, Ottawa needs to be strong and principled — not weak and accommodating.

Given the intense diplomatic animosity caused by the standoff over Meng and the two Michaels, this article references China's demands and malicious punishment tactics, and points out steps that Ottawa must take in dealing with various abuses that China was inflicting on Canada. Every Canadian should be aware of this important chapter in their history.

Canada must develop a backbone in its dealings with China

THE GLOBE AND MAIL, 8 MARCH 2019

CHINA'S SPURIOUS EXCUSE FOR SUSPENDING SOME CANADIAN canola imports this week makes it clear that Ottawa needs to get serious about asserting Canada's interests in diplomatic engagement with this rising global power.

Beijing absurdly claimed that our $2-billion-a-year canola shipments are riddled with weeds that evidently do not even grow in Western Canada.

This isn't about canola. China is resolved to intimidate and coerce Canada, and wants us to realize this beyond any doubt.

Tragically, this diplomatic shambles is partly of our own making, given the horrendous possibility that Michael Kovrig and Michael Spavor, both detained since Dec. 10, could end up in a Chinese prison for life, or even face a death penalty on bogus charges of espionage — all occasioned by Huawei chief financial officer Meng Wanzhou's extradition case.

Beijing bungled things, too, first by assuming Ms. Meng could land in Canada and not be detained under our extradition treaty with the United States, then by misjudging the ability of Prime Minister Justin Trudeau (who they assumed was a charter member of their Canadian pro-China club) to overrule Canada's judicial process.

Now, China wants to abate any loss of face with a succession of get-tough measures that exterminate any goodwill remaining in the avaricious hearts of Canada's business elite and their political friends. On Friday, China's Foreign Minister said that Beijing will take "all necessary measures to resolutely safeguard the legitimate rights and interests of Chinese enterprises and citizens."

The thing is, China no longer wants to comply with the Westphalian system of equal sovereign countries that underlies a rules-based international order, and that is hard for Ottawa to accept. Mr. Trudeau was seriously misled when he thought China would accede to international standards on environmental, gender and labour rights to get a trade deal with a Group of Seven country, but none of his incompetent advisers suffered any consequences for the ensuing fiasco.

Ottawa's feckless appeal to Beijing's moral decency over the Chinese fentanyl manufacturers, whose product kills thousands of Canadians, was met with a Chinese demand to allow a police liaison officer to be installed in China's Vancouver consulate — a request that was rejected over national-security concerns. This impudence squares with Beijing's insistence that Canada allow Huawei equipment to run our telecommunications networks even though China fiercely restricts foreign components in its telecom systems.

Canada must change the channel, immediately. The current dynamic is poisonous to future Canada-China relations, and damages our credibility with our allies, including the United States.

We made a good start by removing John McCallum as ambassador, who seemed to believe that defending Chinese interests in Canada was as important as representing Canadian interests in China. We need someone who actually understands non-democratic kleptocratic regimes, someone who is fluent in a Chinese language to reach beyond the Foreign Ministry gatekeepers and engage directly with China's power-holders. Would we send an ambassador to Washington to engage Congress who could not speak English?

Ottawa missed a huge opportunity when it learned that China was blatantly violating the Vienna Convention on Diplomatic Relations by pressing Michael Kovrig, under severe duress. Mr. Kovrig would have been party to confidential files as part of the Five Eyes intelligence consortium when he had served as a Canadian diplomat. We should have immediately expelled some of the large cohort of Chinese security agents operating semi-openly in Canada.

But again, by our own design, CSIS is weak and misinformed on China. The best we could do was a pathetic exhortation to "please cease and desist." This only inspired Beijing to play harder at saving face over their failure to repatriate Ms. Meng safely away from tough U.S. questions about Huawei's relationship with China's intelligence apparatus.

Canadian law-enforcement agencies have established that the fentanyl that is killing Canadians is almost entirely from southern China factories, sent here via shipping containers or in the mail. Surely we must have the spine to initiate slow, thorough inspections of all Chinese mail and shipments into Canada, until Beijing takes serious, verifiable measures to address this scourge on our national well-being.

We also need to stop laundering, through Canadian casinos and urban real estate, the corrupt earnings by persons associated with senior levels of China's Communist Party. We have laws that address this sort of thing, we need to enforce them.

And we can no longer stand idly by as China detains a million or more Uyghurs in its cultural genocide "re-education" internment camps.

We have a Magnitsky law list of gross violators of human rights who are unwelcome in Canada. Why are there no Chinese names on it?

Canada's years of appeasing China's Communist regime, in the hope of obtaining economic favour, has led us to this horrendous mess. We must regain Canadian self-respect in our relations with China, by honest reassessment and a reboot to get it right.

Viewed against the relentless Meng/Michaels standoff, this item offers a clear if stark sense of Beijing's mindset and tactics as China methodically steamrolls Canada and other middle-powers in its steadily emerging confrontation with the U.S. for global supremacy.

China-Canada tensions are no passing storm

OTTAWA CITIZEN, 1 MAY 2019

AS TIME PASSES SINCE CHINA ARBITRARILY and brutally detained Michael Kovrig and Michael Spavor, sentenced Lloyd Schellenberg to death and severed Canada's $2.7-billion annual canola seed exports, it is clear that our crisis with China is not simply a blip in Beijing's international relations with the West, a Canada-China storm that will eventually calm.

This week, Canadian citizen Fan Wei was sentenced to death in a Chinese drug trial where nine co-accused received lighter sentences.

We are witnessing the early steps of a geo-strategic campaign to eradicate the rules-based international order that sustains Canada and like-minded middle powers against the anarchy of superpower rivalry between China and the United States. If sinking the United Nations and the World Trade Organization is required to achieve this, Beijing will proceed accordingly.

So the federal government politely urging Beijing to grant visas to our agricultural specialists to show the Chinese that our canola seeds are not contaminated as they falsely claim, or seeking mildly supportive press releases from Australia, the Netherlands, Latvia, Lithuania, Estonia, Spain, Denmark — and even from more significant actors such as the European Union, NATO, the United Kingdom, France, Germany and, oh yes, the United States — is evidently not going to get us anywhere.

Canada's days of virtue-signalling are long past the point of getting Kovrig and Spavor out of the hell they endure. China has a million or more Turkic Muslims in "re-education" cultural genocide camps in the PRC's northwest, and plans to do the same to Tibetans. Moreover, there are huge numbers of China's own political prisoners suffering at least as badly in conditions similar to the "black jail" incarceration of our two citizens. In this light, Canadian concerns are unlikely to be very high on the agenda of China's Communist leadership.

In 2012, when Canada thought that free trade with China would be the key to sustainable diversified Canadian prosperity, then-Liberal MP Justin Trudeau put forth that "we deceive ourselves by thinking that trade with Asia can be squeezed into the 20th-century mould. China, for one, sets its own rules and will continue to do so because it can. China has a game plan. There is nothing inherently sinister about that."

But the practice of most Western nations, to condemn politically while engaging economically, has enabled China to make divide-and-conquer an art form. While many of the nations listed above have issued statements supporting Canada's outrage at China's flaunting of international law, most countries remain silent, fearing Beijing's retaliation. In the final analysis, China wields raw money power and the myth that a windfall is coming if Beijing gets what it wants.

Dishonest coercive intimidation is not a traditional Confucian cultural virtue. China succeeds in its existential threat to pluralistic, democratic and free-thinking societies because we have been blinded by greed, and have willingly looked away for more than 25 years as Communist authorities ignored international norms of human rights and fair trade. As a liberal democracy, Canada cannot and would not retaliate in kind by subjecting Huawei CFO Meng Wanzhou to the inhumane treatment meted out to Kovrig and Spavor, or barring Chinese imports through blatantly false claims.

Today, there is growing coordination between security agencies of our allies, seeking to come to terms with Chinese covert activities throughout the world. But just having our own governments' secretive institutions reach consensus on the nature of the problem does not lead to solutions.

We need to relate much better to ethnic Chinese communities in our midst, and see through distorted perceptions that lead to anti-Chinese racism. We urgently need a reset on how Western governments and society deals with China, and we need to do it transparently. Currently, there is no coherent multi-national strategy against Chinese influence operations. The less we respond to it in any substantive way, the more China is emboldened in its practice of global disruption.

China's remaking of the global rules is making the world safe for autocracy, tacitly demanding that Canada passively surrender our values to an authoritarian state. Canada should be uniting with our allies in a coordinated stand for political justice and fair economic engagement with China. But this requires more than allocating resources and government expenditure. The political will has to be there.

Canadians need to be a lot more aware and a lot more determined than we are now, and demand that our politicians do the right thing for Canada and the world.

The world had yet to grasp the full devastation of COVID. Beijing was angrily denying accusations that it withheld or distorted critical information about the virus's Chinese origins. Ottawa continued to avoid banning China's widely-condemned tech giant Huawei. Then the Canadian public delivered a resounding verdict of its own.

In Canada, the tide of opinion is turning on China

THE GLOBE AND MAIL, 21 MAY 2020

IN WHAT SHOULD BE A WAKE-UP call for the federal government, the Canadian public's perception of China appears to be swinging dramatically.

An Angus Reid poll last week found four in five Canadians want Huawei banned from any role in building this country's 5G network, and just 11 per cent of respondents felt Canada should focus its trade efforts on China — down from 40 per cent in 2015. And 76 per cent said Canada should prioritize human rights and the rule of law over economic opportunity.

If Ottawa has been delaying a decision all these months while it awaits the "right moment" to announce that the future of Canadian telecommunications lies with Huawei, it is now clear that moment will never come.

Our government continues to behave as if Canada-China relations will resume status quo ante once the matter of Huawei chief financial officer Meng Wanzhou is resolved. Earlier this year, when Foreign Affairs Minister François-Philippe Champagne chose an adviser for the Asia-Pacific file, he named Pascale Massot, a former senior mentor to Mr. Champagne's predecessor Stéphane Dion. Mr. Dion was the architect of Canada's failed policy of strategic appeasement with Russia, China, Iran and Saudi Arabia. There is no indication Ms. Massot has undergone any Damascene conversion on how best to engage the People's Republic of China.

Last month, Canadian Minister of Health Patty Hajdu, consistent with her party's line, vigorously defended the credibility of the PRC's actions and reporting of COVID-19 cases, insisting, "there is no indication that the data that came out of China in terms of their infection rate and their death rate was falsified in any way." She then told the reporter questioning her on this that they were "feeding into conspiracy theories that many people have been perpetuating on the internet." A lot of us must be deceived by the conspiracy, as the Angus Reid poll found 85 per cent of respondents believe Beijing has not been honest about what happened in its own country regarding the novel coronavirus.

Certainly, China's aggressive new "wolf warrior" diplomacy has the attention of Canadians. Lu Shaye, China's former envoy in Ottawa, suggested last January that Canada and its Western allies were displaying white supremacy by calling for the release of two Canadians imprisoned since December 2018 without any coherent charges. Mr. Lu's ridiculous, highly offensive blathering obviously went over well in Beijing, as he has since been promoted to China's ambassador to France.

In a Global TV interview on Sunday, Mr. Lu's successor, Cong Peiwu, linked the arrests of Michael Kovrig and Michael Spavor — who have been denied any form of consular access (including by phone or video) since January — to the detainment of Ms. Meng, who faces extradition to the United States. Mr. Cong also refuted suggestions that the Chinese Communist Party has been intimidating or bullying its critics.

If the party has been bullying its critics, it's not a new tactic in the grand scheme of its political activities. A report released in March by the Canadian Coalition on Human Rights in China and Amnesty International Canada included details of an apparent intimidation program targeting the Chinese diaspora in Canada.

Last week, Canada's ambassador in Beijing, Dominic Barton, made headlines after he candidly told members of the Canadian International Council that China is alienating other countries by accumulating "negative" soft power in response to international criticism over its handling of the COVID-19 pandemic. Indeed, the response from the PRC has been both defensive and irrational.

Regrettably, the impact of this disease has led to episodes of ugly racism in Canada against Chinese-Canadians. Obviously ethnic Chinese people in Canada have no connection to the Chinese Communist Party's alleged false reporting on the spread of the virus, which has claimed more than 300,000 lives globally. It should be a government priority that any race-based persecution in Canada is met with the full force of Canadian law.

As for Mr. Barton, while it is not his place to set Canada's China policy (an ambassador's job is to implement Canadian foreign policy), Prime Minister Justin Trudeau has implied support for what Mr. Barton said. The fact that he hasn't been fired for speaking out of turn — like his predecessor, John McCallum — offers some hope that this government will finally do the China-policy reset voters seem to have an appetite for.

On the second anniversary of the Spavor and Kovrig detentions, this item examines the fierce China–Canada diplomatic standoff through a chronological review of missteps all along the way by both countries.

Kovrig and Spavor's two-year ordeal and what it means for Canada–China relations

VANCOUVER SUN, 10 DECEMBER 2020

THE ARBITRARY, BRUTAL INCARCERATION OF MICHAEL Spavor and Michael Kovrig in Chinese prison hell is about to enter its third year. This horrendous fiasco is indicative of what is going agonizingly wrong in China's relations with the West.

The ignorant hubris of the Chinese Communist Party's ignoble leaders makes them culpable for the deep suffering of these innocent Canadians. But Ottawa has also mismanaged the situation due to its own misconceptions and lack of willingness to meet this challenge.

This entire saga can be understood as a cascading series of miscalculations. The first was the PRC authorities allowing the Huawei CFO to travel to Canada at all. The U.S. warrant for Meng Wanzhou's arrest had been issued for months. China felt the Canadian elite were sufficiently co-opted by PRC interests that Canada would never act on this extradition request. Evidently, they thought wrong.

After a week of impatient but futile entreaties by the Chinese Embassy, it was apparent Meng's extradition process would proceed. Likely most worrying for Communist officials was the risk that she could reveal Huawei's rumoured connections with the PRC's security and military intelligence apparatus. Presumably to forestall that, Kovrig and Spavor were kidnapped by agents of the Chinese Ministry of State Security and subjected to psychologically torturous conditions.

Here again China appears to have miscalculated. Beijing would have expected the disappearance of two relatively obscure Canadians to initially pressure Ottawa but to ultimately be forgotten. China's Communist leaders didn't expect the detainment of Kovrig and Spavor to emerge as the dominant, intractable issue in Canada-China relations.

China also assumed that its subsequent efforts at economic and trade coercion would convince Canada to release Meng, again demonstrating its misunderstanding of Canada's legal and political systems. China wrongly thought bullying through diplomatic channels — its "wolf-warrior" diplomacy — would make Canada submit.

But Canada did send mixed messages that encouraged Chinese aggression. Highly regrettably, some Canadians tried to appease the Communists by calling for Meng's release. These retired Canadian politicians and civil servants gave China the mistaken impression that they wielded power in Ottawa, which emboldened Beijing.

China was further encouraged by the persistent weakness of the governing Liberals. By not meeting China's challenges, Ottawa communicated that aggression would be met with passivity. With no direct consequences, China believed its belligerence would yield dividends. On this point it was also wrong.

Not only has Canada, to its credit, refused to release Meng, but now only seven per cent of Canadians have a positive impression of China. Huawei, which at one point appeared likely to get the nod to develop

Canada's 5G, no longer has a viable telecom partner in Canada. And opposition politicians have seized upon this moment to strengthen calls for a serious, principled foreign policy toward China.

Beijing has so far failed to secure Meng's release and, for virtually all Canadians except those around the cabinet table, the jig is up; Canadians now understand, and distrust, China.

U.S. President Elect Joe Biden could complicate Beijing's predicament, as his stated goals of confronting China multilaterally will seriously limit Beijing's ability to pick on smaller states. A U.S.-led multilateral strategy will make weakness from Ottawa less viable.

Canada must recognize that our relations with China are a function of an integrated Party-state-military-civilian-market PRC regime complex whose strategic intent is severely at odds with our own interests and values. Currently, Canada deals largely with the PRC's Ministry of Foreign Affairs, a weak player in the Chinese system. We should put far more resources into comprehensive engagement with all power elements in China, in the same way we manage relations with the U.S.

It's a necessary but challenging task. Canada still lacks linguistic, cultural and political wherewithal to defend our interests against a very sophisticated engagement by China.

And while Canada's approach to China continues to flounder, Michael Kovrig and Michael Spavor must wonder, day after excruciating day, why nobody turns up to bring them home.

The darkness gets darker. This commentary dissects Beijing's potent combination of political theatre and diplomatic contempt. China's leadership revels in playing the bully and trying to humiliate Canada for adhering to its core principles of justice.

Treatment of the Two Michaels reveals Canada's lack of leverage in Beijing

GLOBAL NEWS, 19 APRIL 2021
(co-authored with Brett Byers)

MICHAEL KOVRIG AND MICHAEL SPAVOR, THE hostages that Beijing infamously abducted in response to the lawful arrest of Huawei CFO Meng Wanzhou, are set to go to "trial."

Yet anyone who knows much about China's legal system already understands the conclusion of the trial has already been determined by the Chinese Communist Party.

The secret sham trials, which Canadian authorities have hitherto failed to secure access to, are another dark step toward a seemingly inevitable conclusion. Chinese courts have a conviction rate of over 99 per cent; cases are often heard in a matter of mere hours; Spavor's trial apparently ended in two hours. It may be some time before the official verdict is public. Yet Kovrig and Spavor, whose only "crime" is being Canadian in the wrong place at the wrong time, could eventually be sentenced to many more years in Chinese prison. The death penalty for espionage is not out of the question, either.

The timing is no accident. Set against a backdrop of bilateral meetings between U.S. and Chinese officials in Anchorage, it is possible the trials are a sort of flex from Beijing ahead of negotiations that could set the tone for Sino-American relations under the Biden administration. Moreover, with Meng's legal team failing to secure her release, her extradition is looking increasingly likely.

What stands out most at this moment is how little leverage or power Canada has. Our response has been downright paltry. Kovrig and Spavor have suffered under torturous conditions with virtually no consular access. By all accounts, the trial announcement came as a surprise for Ottawa. Short of capitulating to China by abandoning our principles around the rule of law and releasing Meng, or hoping for an American-brokered solution, Canada's options at this juncture are incredibly limited.

It did not have to be this way.

China's hostage diplomacy persists because Beijing is encouraged by our weakness. A bully only engages in a shakedown if they believe they will get what they want. By failing to rise to the challenge posed by the Chinese Communist Party (CCP) regime, the decision-makers in Beijing believe that Canada can be coerced.

Instead of sanctioning human rights violators in China, Canada did nothing meaningful. Our government remained timid, simply eliciting anodyne statements from like-minded allies expressing disapproval for arbitrary detention. But Canada was reluctant to reciprocally make common cause with the many other middle powers whose citizens have been similarly victims of China's increasing application of hostage diplomacy coercion. Sooner than making common-sense decisions such as barring Huawei from 5G or opening our doors to Hong Kong refugees, Ottawa looked eager to return to the "business as usual" relationship that China has for decades exploited and abused.

Canada's failure to stand up for itself has all but guaranteed this outcome. Kovrig and Spavor are now facing sham trials and Canada has virtually no leverage. A major reversal in our hitherto passive strategy is necessary if we hope to inspire a better result.

And yet, even failing a solution motivated by concrete Canadian action, there is a thin ray of hope for Kovrig and Spavor. After their conviction, China could well decide that the political price it has paid, including the obliteration of Canadian goodwill towards the People's Republic, does not merit the continuation of this charade.

Beijing could also release Kovrig and Spavor as a fake olive branch designed to trick a new administration in Washington and a weak-willed Canadian government to ignore China's many transgressions. This was the case with Kevin Garratt, another Canadian victim of China's hostage diplomacy, whose release in 2017 just two days after an absurd eight-year sentence was handed down was misread by Ottawa as evidence that Beijing could be reasoned with.

But recent years have given stunning clarity to the true nature of the CCP regime. Petty, vindictive, arbitrary, and brutal, Beijing has made no mystery about its authoritarian intentions. Kovrig and Spavor's plight fits a pattern of belligerence from the regime, including its military incursions and overt threat against its neighbours, genocide against Uyghurs in Xinjiang, blanket repression of cultural, racial, and religious minorities, militarization of international waters in the South China Sea, repression in Hong Kong, and so much more.

Canada's naïveté toward China has left us impotent and rudderless in the face of Beijing's aggression. What is desperately needed is for Ottawa to finally wake up to the reality that Canadians have acknowledged for some time: China is a clear threat that we must be prepared to stand against in concert with our allies.

HUAWEI
AND
CANADA'S 5G SECURITY

Like most of its western allies, Ottawa was grappling with whether or not to let Chinese tech giant Huawei help build Canada's 5G wireless network, due to very credible concerns that Beijing would use the partnership as a path for cyber-espionage.

Weighing Huawei in Canada-China relations

EMBASSY MAGAZINE, 17 OCTOBER 2012

ON OCTOBER 8 (2012), THE PERMANENT Select Committee on Intelligence of the U.S. House of Representatives issued their "Investigative report on the U.S. National Security Issues posed by Chinese Telecommunications Companies Huawei and ZTE", based on a study carried out over 11 months at the behest of Huawei, the world's second-biggest maker of routers, switches and associated telecommunications.

Huawei hoped the study would dispel persistent but unproven allegations that it is a heavily subsidized front company of the Chinese People's Liberation Army and the Chinese Ministry of State Security.

The Select Committee heard hearsay evidence of serious allegations of malfeasance by Huawei (which have been referred to the U.S. Justice Department and the Department of Homeland Security), but it turned up nothing definitive — at least, not in the unclassified part of the report.

However, because there was enough doubt that Huawei "cannot be trusted to be free of foreign state influence and thus pose a threat to the United States and to our systems," Congress imposed severe restrictions on Huawei's future business activities in the U.S.

This compelling report is of high interest in Canada, where Huawei, through highly competitive bids, has won contracts to supply sophisticated data networking equipment to at least Bell, Telus, Sasktel and Wind.

Competitors claim Huawei can offer below-market pricing in its network installations thanks to secret funding it gets from the Chinese government. Regardless of whether that is true, the Select Committee's report suggests that buying Huawei could be a very false economy for Canada.

Some observers were quick to downplay any implications the U.S. report could have for Canada. Telecom analyst Iain Grant has been quoted as saying he is "not sure that the technical judgment of the U.S. Congress is a yardstick that Canadian companies need to consider when making technical decisions. Canadian companies assess the attraction of Huawei gear on its merits, on function, on delivery and timeliness, on quality of what is delivered and on price. Paranoia is not a measure they find germane."

But clearly there are bases for concern about any Huawei equipment processing massive quantities of Canadian data. Certainly, the Government of Canada has already indicated Huawei will be excluded from bidding on a new government digital, telephone, data and e-mail network, on the basis that it is "too dicey to be included in constructing the network."

Among the unproven allegations in the Congressional report is that Huawei routers are able to activate "back door" software that sends data to "an elite cyber-warfare unit within the PLA." Similar routines hidden in millions of line of code could enable China to remotely shut down any Huawei-installed networks for strategic reasons. As technology progresses, the ability to carry out targeted mining of the huge data quantities passing through Huawei-installed Canadian routers and switches, using sophisticated computer algorithms, becomes a greater cause for concern. Moreover, the equipment will require maintenance and "software updates", opening up the possibility of further opportunities for cyber-espionage.

It all comes down to a question of trust. If the Canadian telecommunications project had been prepared to pay more for the Swedish Ericsson or French Alcatel Lucent installations instead, there would be less cause for alarm.

According to the U.S. report, Huawei admits the Chinese Communist Party maintains a Party Committee within the company, but won't explain how the committee functions or even reveal which individuals compose the committee, on the grounds that this information is a Chinese state secret and Huawei could be prosecuted in China if they came clear on this point.

Furthermore, since only People's Republic of China nationals are permitted to own shares in Huawei by company policy, it stands to reason that Huawei's senior management (also citizens) could not ignore a Chinese Party-State order to facilitate cyber-intelligence gathering or "back door" network processes, if couched in Chinese national security terms. (And it would certainly be virtually impossible for buyers of Huawei networks to detect.)

Beyond a doubt, Beijing has shown a strong proclivity to engage in cyber espionage. After the German Chancellery and three ministries were penetrated by hackers, evidently from China, and infected with spyware, Chancellor Angela Merkel stood in public next to Chinese Premier Wen Jiabao and openly criticized his government for its attacks. Canadian government computers also suffered similar assaults just last year, causing considerable disruption to operations.

And what of private-sector customers of Canadian telecommunication companies that use Huawei equipment to carry their data? Should activists for Chinese human rights, or Canadian companies competing for business contracts in China, be concerned? Considering how unforthcoming and obscure Huawei was in its responses to the pertinent questions posed by the U.S. Congress, this is a valid concern.

Unfortunately it appears that, for Canada, it is already too late to second-guess our trust in the honesty and sincerity of this Chinese firm.

European governments had barred Huawei from their telecom networks, and Washington released a scathing report describing a corporate culture of intellectual property theft. But Ottawa continued to dither over what to do. Fed up with waiting for a decision, Canadian telecom companies said they would begin, or prepare to begin, incorporating Huawei components into the country's new 5G networks.

Why Canada can't let Huawei build a 5G network

OTTAWA CITIZEN, 21 FEBRUARY 2020

CANADA'S BIG THREE TELECOM COMPANIES AREN'T waiting for the federal government's ever-delayed Huawei security review. Telus has announced it will forge ahead and install Huawei 5G technology — damn the consequences. Bell will presumably not be far behind, as Rogers has already started to implement 5G service in four Canadian cities using Ericsson technology.

For the federal government, the Huawei decision clock is running out.

On Feb. 13, the U.S. government released a new indictment against Huawei and its CFO, Meng Wanzhou, depicting a corporate culture so corrupt that, besides extensive theft of intellectual property and propriety manufacturing processes by Huawei's own espionage agents, there is even an incentive scheme rewarding employees who upload stolen materials to an encrypted e-mail address, or sneak into rivals' labs and steal devices.

The indictment details Huawei's mendacity, betrayal of commitments and half-hearted attempts to cover it all up by blaming "rogue employees." It also cites Huawei's provision of surveillance technology to Iran, which uses it to monitor, identify and detain protesters (presumably the same kit used against the Xinjiang Uyghurs, and coming soon to Hong Kong and the rest of China).

Washington promises to cut off intelligence-sharing with Canada if we go with the Huawei 5G. Lest anyone think this is merely Donald Trump's "America First" antipathy to China's rising global role, his Democratic nemesis, Nancy Pelosi, implored the recent Munich Security Conference to reject Chinese "digital autocracy through its telecommunication giant Huawei," while a senior U.S. delegation in London pressed Prime Minister Boris Johnson to reverse his decision to give Huawei partial access to British telecommunications.

The debate in Canada swings on whether it is possible to use Huawei technology on the periphery of 5G installations while keeping the core networks secure. It must be determined if the federal Communications Security Establishment can genuinely monitor Huawei hardware and software to ensure the PRC cannot manipulate critical Canadian infrastructure such as power and water, or use Huawei technology to further expand Beijing's well documented cyber-espionage.

Being shut out of U.S. intelligence-sharing would leave Canada even more susceptible to the security threats of Russia (especially in the Arctic) and China (everywhere). But there is another, more fundamental moral factor. Does Canada honestly want to send the profits from billions of dollars of 5G installation to China's Huawei, a dishonest and dissembling corporate entity that is digitally facilitating Xi Jinping's ever strengthening program of political repression?

Here at home, Huawei does have its supporters. Its Canadian employees are understandably trying to put a good face on it, and telecom executives warm to the cheaper price point of Huawei, which is heavily subsidized by the Chinese state. And there is pressure on the Prime Minister's Office from numerous other quarters to put through approval for Huawei's 5G technology.

In New Zealand, a startling report by scholar Anne-Marie Brady to that nation's Parliamentary Inquiry on Foreign Interference details the Chinese Communist Party's massive scheme of enticing foreign politicians, academics and business people to promote China's agenda through political lobbying, the media and academia. Besides offering business opportunities or free trips to China, using bribery or honey traps and so on, there are also "consultancies" in which prominent advisers pocket up to $150,000 per annum just for being affiliated with PRC entities. So long as the foreign adviser promotes relations with China on PRC terms, the money keeps coming.

Back in Ottawa, the new Special Committee on Canada-China Relations needs to seriously explore whether what is happening in New Zealand can happen here. As decision day on Huawei edges nearer, we need legislation requiring transparent reporting of Canadians' income derived from foreign sources. Sunshine is the best disinfectant.

Patience is lapsing for Canada's indecision over Huawei. The government needs to take a stand, once and for all, on the security threat of Huawei 5G. The real question is: Why would any disinterested party think that going with Huawei 5G is the right thing for Canada?

In light of Russia's expansionist invasion of Ukraine, and China's expected reprisal after Ottawa banned Huawei from Canada's data networks, this commentary examines the Canadian government's history of dysfunctionality when it comes to compelling Canada's secretive security agencies to provide MPs with security briefings so that Parliament can craft legislation to confront foreign interference. This article gives examples of past failures and prescribes what Ottawa could be doing instead of clinging to a culture of terminal inaction and "no further comment".

Canada must boost its security apparatus against China and Russia

OTTAWA CITIZEN, 25 MAY 2022

THE FEDERAL GOVERNMENT'S DECISION TO BAN Chinese telecom giant Huawei from working on Canada's 5G network will certainly lead to economic retaliation from China, but we will not be coerced into reversing the decision. Ever since Russia launched its barbaric assault on Ukraine, Canada has shown a new determination to protect our sovereignty and national security from the malign schemes of Beijing or the Kremlin.

The Russian and Chinese regimes have always been incompatible with democracy, but Canadians' awareness of this has been sharpened by recent events. Vladimir Putin — angry and resentful over his humiliating Ukrainian miscalculation — is dangerously capable of lashing out at Canada and our NATO allies. He will undoubtedly strengthen his bond with China, sharing an anti-western agenda that emphasizes espionage, sabotage and even attacks on our critical infrastructure.

Canada is not adequately prepared, and has to get moving on some urgent matters.

Besides rapidly making up for decades of neglect of our Arctic defences, we must find ways to get Canadian oil and gas to Europe as expeditiously as possible. The new federal budget promised meaningful action to ensure Canada is not left beholden to China for critical minerals that our high-tech future depends on, but we need to do much more to protect our global supply chains.

Our vulnerability was revealed with Beijing's sanctions against canola seeds and meat during the Meng Wanzhou fiasco, and the unconscionable detention of Michael Kovrig and Michael Spavor. There is no basis for Canada to trust Russia or China, be it in trade, climate change cooperation, or in the UN. It is time for us to do a comprehensive reset of our foreign policy doctrine.

A major concern is whether the RCMP, the Canadian Security Intelligence Service (CSIS), the Department of National Defence and the Communications Security Establishment (CSE) routinely shroud their accountability to Canadians and Parliament. We know these agencies gather a lot of information on Russian and Chinese malign activities, but when Parliament asks for a briefing to inform the development of legislation to protect public safety and national security, those agencies too often obfuscate, claiming their information is too sensitive to share with MPs or that disclosing it would reveal operational details that would help our enemies.

Canada can learn much from Australia, Britain, the U.S. and Scandinavian countries in terms of drawing the line between withholding information that threatens national security versus security agencies simply exaggerating classification protocols to evade accountability for their shortcomings.

For example, how badly does Canada need a foreign agents registry act, or something like the Australian Foreign Influence Transparency Scheme Act, as a national security measure? In today's environment, such protection is crucial for Canada, and CSIS should know which persons influential in Canada's policy process have received benefits from a foreign state that put them in a conflict of interest and threaten Canadian security and sovereignty. In 2010, then-CSIS Director Richard Fadden made headlines by revealing that cabinet ministers in two provinces, and several municipal politicians, were influenced by a foreign government when making policy decisions. But evidently nothing was done about it at the time or since. Twelve years on, how many more policymakers are under the influence of a foreign power today? How high does it go? If CSIS is doing its job, it has this data.

Consider Cameron Ortis, former director general of the RCMP's national intelligence unit, who was accused in 2019 of trying to share sensitive information with a foreign entity. What should we be learning from his arrest? Or the Winnipeg labs matter? Was there a failure to protect national security that should be addressed by Parliament? Then there's Quentin Huang. Charged in 2013 with trying to sell Canadian military secrets to China, the Canadian engineer went eight years without a trial before a judge finally dismissed the case, citing lack of progress. Why is it that, unlike our allies, Canada is incapable of holding a proper trial of someone accused of transferring our military technologies to a foreign state?

If the RCMP, CSIS and CSE refuse to share intelligence assessments on where Canada is vulnerable to Russian and Chinese malign operations, the federal government must take the required steps to defend our security. Too often, Canadian police and security agencies see their role as simply curating information that they can trade with the counterpart agencies. This danger is much more pronounced in Canada than among our allies, whose security agencies have much more effective legislative oversight.

The suffering of Ukraine is not just bad weather in international relations; it's the harbinger of geostrategic climate change led by China as well. Canada must cut the rhetoric and take action to face the new global realities.

THE
CORONAVIRUS

In the Chinese city of Wuhan, a strange pneumonia was claiming more and more lives. North Americans were initially unconcerned about this virus over in Asia, but within weeks countries around the world were in lockdown as sickness and death spread to every continent. As governments rushed to evacuate their nationals from China, Beijing mysteriously delayed allowing Canada's rescue aircraft to land. COVID would claim 3.4 million lives.

Many concerns as Canadians wait for evacuation from China

TORONTO STAR, 4 FEBRUARY 2020

WHILE THOUSANDS OF PEOPLE FROM COUNTRIES around the world were flown out of China in the past week, seeking sanctuary from Wuhan coronavirus, some 325 Canadians continued to wait for Chinese authorities to let an aircraft land in Wuhan and evacuate them.

The United States, Japan, South Korea, Jordan, Britain, Portugal, Bangladesh and Indonesia have all got their nationals out in recent days. Ottawa has chartered aircraft on standby, but officials in Beijing have not said when the flights would be allowed to land. At a Monday press conference about plans for evacuating Canadians from Wuhan, cabinet ministers Francois-Philippe Champagne (Global Affairs), Patty Hajdu

(Health) and Harjit Singh (National Defence) were unable to suggest when China might allow a Canadian airplane to land.

Dark questions remain around the delay. Regular flights to Wuhan airport are suspended, so evidently air space and loading facilities are not a problem. Surely the People's Republic of China would not leverage the well-being of ordinary Canadians against the political crisis engendered by the detention of Huawei CFO Meng Wanzhou. If that proved to be the case, Ottawa would need to deeply reconsider Canada's relations with China once the crisis is under control.

The coronavirus outbreak has led to unprecedented global efforts to contain the virus and minimize its cost in human lives.

As was the case with SARS, the Wuhan coronavirus has been linked to the sale of live wildlife at a public market, this one in Wuhan. China has thousands of such markets, selling tanks of crabs and live fish as well as butchered pork, beef, lamb and live chickens slaughtered and plucked for you on the spot. They also sell caged live snakes, turtles, guinea pigs, badgers, cats and dogs, even wolf cubs.

These spectacles provide fascination for foreign tourists, but scientific experts characterize China's "wet markets" as perfect incubators for novel pathogens. There is a lot of urine and feces blowing about in a confined atmosphere.

The question is, 17 years after SARS claimed hundreds of lives in China and around the world, what have Chinese health authorities been doing to keep workers in these markets safe from serious disease? Evidently not enough.

There is a serious lack of confidence regarding information out of China about what is really going on. Consider the fiasco of suppression of medical workers in Wuhan who, weeks ago, detected the return of a SARS-like respiratory disease. When they took to social media to alert medical colleagues, these doctors found themselves detained by the police for "spreading rumours." Even the Mayor of Wuhan is defending his lack of timely response by claiming that central authorities in Beijing refused to allow Wuhan to initiate measures that might have confined the spread.

One thing China's authoritarian dictatorship has done a superb job with is preventing movement around the country, blocking all forms of public and private transportation out of affected areas, which now extend beyond Hubei Province to pockets all over China.

This lockdown is also a worry for people around the world who have been attempting to send relief parcels into the trouble spots. Like many Canadians with friends and family in China, I recently shipped a big box of medical supplies from St. Catharines. We were not confident it would arrive at the intended address, given the current chaos and desperation.

To our relief, the authorities are giving priority handling to medical shipments from abroad, and it did show up at an enormous warehouse filled with similar packages from around the world.

Many well-informed experts say Beijing's official numbers for both coronavirus infections and deaths are grossly underestimated, by up to a factor of 35. But it is hard to know, and that is the point. Many people are dying at home, without access to treatment at overburdened hospitals. Few in China believe the government's statements. Policies of strategic deception are encoded in the Chinese Communist Party's DNA.

For many Chinese the anxiety grows daily, trapped in their homes, afraid to go out and lacking supplies of surgical masks or food supplies. In the meantime, party General Secretary Xi Jinping appears to have gone to ground, vanishing from his dominance in the media, his political future evidently uncertain.

As Chinese officials backpedalled and covered up absurd early denials about COVID — which by now was killing millions globally — a more sinister question arose: Did politically defensive misinformation issued by Beijing, and relayed to the world, lead to massive numbers of unnecessary deaths and global economic hardship? This article examines Beijing's history of making face-saving but ultimately farcical claims that few in the world believed.

Beijing's coronavirus bungling makes Canada's choice on Huawei even easier

THE GLOBE AND MAIL, 22 APRIL 2020

LAST WEEK, CHINESE PRESIDENT XI JINPING'S government acknowledged that the numbers it originally cited for coronavirus deaths in Wuhan had been under-reported by 50 per cent. Foreign ministry spokesman Zhao Lijian said the virus's rapid spread had contributed to undercounting, and insisted this was not a cover-up: "We'll never allow any concealment."

This assertion is certainly belied by foreign intelligence briefings. As Steve Tsang, of the China Institute at the University of London, put it, "The statistics have been changed most probably because the old figures were so ridiculous that even the Communist Party Propaganda

Department knows it was unsustainable. Hence, a revision to a level less incredible, but one that will still present the Party under Xi as having done a vastly better job than Western democratic governments."

Moreover, an earlier absurd statement by Mr. Zhao – that COVID-19 may have been brought to China by U.S. participants in last October's controversial World Military Games held in Wuhan – suggests that China's leaders likely know something they desperately want to hide about the origins and spread of this pandemic, and are panicking by disseminating ludicrous propaganda.

Looking back, many governments grappling with the pandemic would have responded differently if they'd known then what they know now. As late as March 6, Canadian health officials were saying the risk posed by coronavirus in this country remained low. U.S. President Donald Trump's early missteps have proven tragically disastrous for our American friends. We weep for the people of Italy, Spain, France and the U.K., whose governments could have responded much sooner.

So, the question looms: Did politically motivated misinformation issued by Beijing, and uncritically relayed to the world via the WHO, lead to massive numbers of unnecessary deaths and economic hardship around the world?

The People's Republic of China insists it offered honest and timely data about the spread of this virus in China and abroad, but the facts on the ground – including the persecution and disappearances of brave citizens who tried to get the truth out, and the Communist Party's historical reluctance in moments like the 2003 SARS epidemic to acknowledge facts unfavourable to their rule – strongly suggest otherwise.

This is the same regime that insisted "not one person died on Tiananmen Square;" who state that a million Uyghurs are happy to be in crowded prison camps, forbidden from practising their religion, because there they have an opportunity for vocational training and learning Mandarin Chinese; who claim that people in Taiwan yearn to give up their hard-won democracy in favour of being ruled by a one-party autocracy out of Beijing.

This is the same regime, indeed, that claimed that Kevin and Julia Garratt, Michael Spavor, and Michael Kovrig are spies in service of Canadian dark forces. And that Canadian canola shipments are so full of contaminants that billions of dollars of PRC export contracts must be cancelled indefinitely.

Canada faces difficult decisions about how to restore its economy after the pandemic, including the long-stalled one on whether to let Chinese telecom Huawei into our 5G network. H.R. McMaster, the former U.S. National Security Advisor whose credibility is enhanced by having been fired by Mr. Trump (Gen. McMaster called the President "a dope"), recently indicated that many Huawei workers are simultaneously employed by China's Ministry of State Security and the intelligence arm of the People's Liberation Army.

The U.K., Australia, France and the United States have called for an international investigation of the PRC and WHO's apparent mismanagement of the COVID-19 pandemic. If China were found culpable, would Canada still accept Beijing's assurance that Huawei poses no threat to the security of Canadian 5G infrastructure, or that China will not seek to use it to further its cyber-espionage program in Canada? And in the background, of course, is China's broad disregard for international rules-based order in trade and diplomacy.

Canada must carefully evaluate the extent to which we can engage with China economically, and whether that would require compromising our national security or conceding an "if you can't beat them, join them" abandonment of Canadian support for justice, fairness, reciprocity and human rights. While our front line health workers work heroically to stave off more tragic death, we should spend our isolation weighing our own integrity.

Although China was clearly the epicentre of COVID-19's emergence, the Beijing regime was globally criticized after it sought to minimize reporting and restrict information sharing with governments that were scrambling to manage the public health disaster. The pandemic would go on to claim over three million lives worldwide.

Holding China to account for the COVID-19 coverup

INSIDE POLICY, 26 MAY 2020
(co-authored with Brett Byers)

AS THE COVID-19 PANDEMIC CONTINUES TO unfold, it is clear that it has already caused untold economic and human suffering. While battling the present crisis must be the priority at this point, soon there will be a need to hold accountable those whose actions allowed the novel coronavirus to spread from Wuhan last fall to grow into a global pandemic.

As evidence mounts and the timeline becomes clearer, it is increasingly apparent that the government of China knew what was going on with this disease early on and chose to cover up, obfuscate, and suppress the truth about COVID-19. Authorities in Wuhan were informed about the human-to-human transmission of COVID-19, including to its medical personnel, and the exponential increase of infections in the province as early as December 2019 – and for political reasons they chose to ignore and refute such warnings.

Indeed, Taiwan, a country whose successful management of the crisis is so far without parallel, had also determined that there was human-to-human transmission in Wuhan as early as December of 2019. Taiwan reported this to the World Health Organization (WHO) despite being excluded from even observer status in the WHO due to Beijing's political demands to shun Taiwan at the UN. Taiwan was able to act almost three weeks before China publicly admitted there was human-to-human transmission.

Rather than moving to contain the crisis, local Chinese Communist Party (CCP) officials were more concerned with arresting and forcing false confessions from doctors and journalists who raised alarm bells. They also interfered to prevent hospitals from notifying central health authorities about the seriousness of the outbreak.

Indeed, China had created an infectious disease reporting after the 2002 SARS crisis to prevent such political meddling, yet it abjectly failed its very first test. This should not be surprising given the propensity of Chinese Communist officials to ignore or deny anything that reflects negatively on the regime.

It was also not solely the fault of the Hubei provincial government. Even after it was informed of the seriousness of the outbreak, Asian news media reported that China's National Health Commission had "ordered institutions not to publish any information related to the unknown disease, and ordered labs to transfer any samples they had to designated testing institutions, or to destroy them."

Due to this official silence, millions were able to leave Hubei before the belated government lockdown, thereby helping to spread this virus throughout China and globally. The world was left in the dark on both the scale of the COVID-19 epidemic in China and its broader dangers.

The fact is, China lied in an aggressive, systematic, and pervasive fashion. Every lie told to the WHO and the world at large only reduced the ability of governments around the world to adequately prepare and respond to the crisis leading to massive rates of unnecessary deaths from COVID-19

There is evidence that, had China taken concrete action when Taiwan started acting, global infections (and therefore deaths) could have been reduced by up to 95 per cent. China's culpability for the initial spread of the virus and its role in fostering an ill-prepared global community is beyond a shadow of a doubt.

The world's governments must hold China to account.

There are plenty of actions that Canada should be taking immediately, in coordination with our allies and partners, in direct response to China's lethal COVID-19 coverup.

First, Magnitsky sanctions should be considered for those officials who are found to be responsible for lying about COVID-19. These sanctions are designed to financially target specific individuals who are responsible for human rights abuses. As the WHO's constitution states, "the enjoyment of the highest attainable standard of health is one of the fundamental rights of every human being," meaning a case can be made under Magnitsky legislation.

Second, Canada should also support Taiwan's observer status in the WHO, its participation in the World Health Assembly, and its meaningful involvement in all manner of other important international fora, including trade agreements like the CPTPP. Taiwan has proven itself to be a valuable, constructive global partner. We should no longer allow China's political preferences to supersede international cooperation with Taiwan. And, had the world acted in accordance with the China-skepticism embodied by Taiwan, perhaps this crisis would have never become such a disastrous pandemic.

Third, countries should reassess their economic reliance on China and should actively encourage supply chain diversification away from

China, particularly with regard to medical supplies and strategic resources like rare earth elements. Countries should consider divesting from the Asia Infrastructure Investment Bank and should seek to provide alternative development financing for countries that otherwise might be swayed by China's Belt and Road Initiative.

There can be no question that the Government of China must be held accountable for the spread of COVID-19. This is by no means an exhaustive list of available tactics that would be effective in undermining Beijing's strategic interests in a major way and send a clear message to China that its flouting of the international rules based order has serious consequences.

CANADA'S SOVEREIGNTY vs CHINA AND TRUMP

If this 2017 discussion seems familiar, it may be because it was eerily prophetic to Donald Trump's tariff threats / trade war that haunted the world when he returned to the White House in 2025. For Canada and other nations seeking new markets, China also inevitably enters the discussion. We have been down this road before.

As Trump roils, Ottawa shuffles the deck to play a new China card

ST. CATHARINES (ONT.) STANDARD, 31 JANUARY 2017

WITH WASHINGTON AND CHINA BICKERING INTO diplomatic chill, the Justin Trudeau government is angling to be viewed in Beijing as a friendly face alongside a hostile, nationalistic Donald Trump.

Given Trump's vow to tear up NAFTA and rewrite it in America's favour, no doubt meaning new tariffs on Canadian goods and services, Ottawa is apparently looking to offset the hit by accessing new Chinese markets and removing the restrictions of Chinese state investment in Canada.

But any move to initiate free trade talks with China has serious geopolitical implications. For instance, by further integrating into Canada's economy, China gains influence in a nation on the U.S. border.

Meantime, John McCallum's recent appointment as Canada's ambassador in Beijing suggests Ottawa is serious about upgrading relations. China regards McCallum as "a friend," and knows he is a former senior minister with a direct line to the Prime Minister's Office, so he'll be accorded high-level access by Beijing.

With global political axes in flux, it's a good time for Canada to assess where we have been with China, and what future Canada-China relations should look like. But Ottawa needs to keep eyes wide open as it considers the costs and benefits of greater economic dependence on China.

In the early years of Canada-China relations, led by Pierre Trudeau, many Canadians sympathized with Mao Zedong, who was seen as achieving social justice and cultural revolution on Chinese terms. But after Mao's death in 1976, perspectives changed. The "Great Proletarian Cultural Revolution Campaign" became "10 years of disaster," and Canadian public opinion began favouring China's transit to a more democratic path. Hundreds of millions of dollars from the Canadian International Development Agency went to train Chinese judges in rule of law, align China with universal norms of human rights, and bring its laws and practices into compliance with the UN International Covenant on Civil and Political Rights.

Today it is clear that none of it led anywhere, and repression continues unabated. But in those days, the English-speaking, tennis-partner Chinese government "friends" of senior western diplomats urged us to be patient, stay the course — and keep the cash coming. Their "old comrades" just needed time to adjust to China's moving away from Leninism, but change was coming. Political reform was always just over the horizon, and Canada's support during the transition would be rewarded.

In telexes back to their governments, diplomats characterized these "friends" as "progressive agents of change," but in retrospect they were simply agents of the Communist Party Central Committee, mandated to cultivate "useful idiots" who would facilitate Beijing's interests to foreign countries. We were flimflammed into hearing what we wanted to hear. The spectre of riches for businesses friendly to Beijing led us to forgive China's unfair trade practices, human rights abuses and support for dictators in Asia, Africa and South America.

Things changed in 2013 when Xi Jinping came to power as a vigorous strongman, forcefully repudiating any notions that China would liberalize. The Cultural Revolution was no longer called "10 years of disaster," for the party has always done the right thing in the context of the times. Discussion of "universal values," "Western bourgeois democracy," "freedom of expression," "independent judiciary" and so on — in print, online, in universities or party think tanks — became verboten.

Today, Xi Jinping's regime is militarily aggressive and much more demanding of nations where China has established economic leverage through strategic trade and investment agreements.

Meanwhile, Beijing's clashes with a Trump administration bring new clarity to the incompatibilities between the political systems of Beijing and the West.

More China in the Canadian economy appears to be Canada's future as the U.S. lapses into protectionism. In trying to negotiate a free trade with China, a key issue for Canada will be, do we have to negotiate away our commitment to Canadian liberal and democratic values to get the deal?

Deep into his first term as president, Donald Trump continued to confound longtime American allies as he made concessions to dictators who represent clear threats to democratic freedom. In this instance, Trump's courting of Xi Jinping left Canada twisting in the wind.

How Xi trumped Trump at the G20 summit

THE GLOBE AND MAIL, 30 JUNE 2019

DONALD TRUMP MET WITH CHINA'S SUPREME leader Xi Jinping for 80 minutes at the G20 summit in Osaka on Friday. For Canada, the meeting wasn't good — but it was for China.

While China's long-term preparations for its new cold war confrontation with the U.S. continue apace, Mr. Trump's infatuation of autocratic dictators — of which Mr. Xi is primus inter pares — shows no signs of abating. At the press conference following their meeting, Mr. Trump told a Chinese reporter that Mr. Xi is "a brilliant leader. He's a brilliant man. You know better than I, he is probably considered to be one of the great leaders of 200 years in China."

There was no mention of Mr. Xi's leadership over Chinese Communist Party policies which have incarcerated 3 million Uyghurs (the figure used by the U.S. State Department) under harsh conditions in cultural genocide camps. Mr. Trump indicated that Hong Kong also didn't come up.

In their meeting, Mr. Xi made shrewd inroads, deferring new tariffs on US$300 billion worth of exports to the U.S. with the usual promises of "dialogue," vague commitments to co-operate on the threats of Iran and North Korea, and talk of large purchases of U.S. agricultural and other goods.

Mr. Trump, meanwhile, was agreeing to reconsider security restrictions on Chinese researchers entering the U.S., and to end the current ban on American company sales to Huawei.

Mr. Xi made no concessions on non-tariff barriers to access to the Chinese market, or on espionage — including covert, coercive or corrupt purloining of U.S. technologies to serve China's larger interests. So, China's plan to control global telecommunications through Huawei will continue unaffected.

For all this, Mr. Trump called the outcome "better than expected." It makes you wonder what he expected.

Canada certainly seems no closer to getting Michael Kovrig and Michael Spavor out of the hell of Chinese custody. Apparently this matter and Huawei CFO Meng Wanzhou's arrest were not even raised, so any moral appeal that Prime Minister Justin Trudeau may have tried on Mr. Trump in Washington last month was for naught.

Canada's tough situation with China is not helped by former Prime Minister Jean Chrétien publicly urging Ottawa to quash Ms. Meng's extradition hearing, or former ambassador John McCallum (in his new role as middleman for Canada-China business) pressuring Ottawa to push the U.S. to just drop the fraud charges against Ms. Meng.

China's latest anti-Canada aggression — banning Canadian meat imports — was likely fanned by Beijing's perception that Mr. Chrétien and Mr. McCallum's business-backed urging might bring about Ms. Meng's release, especially if backed up by PRC intimidation.

Here at home, the Conservatives promise a reset on China policy if they win the fall election, but what about the Liberals doing a rethink on it right now? Canadian foreign policy should not be reduced to partisan political football. We evidently got it very wrong on China before, so let's get it right in Canada's national interest now. The time for giving in to our naiveté and greed is now long past.

As to the larger question of China's hegemonic global ambitions, U.S. farmers will be delighted about getting their China market back, thanks to Mr. Xi and Mr. Trump's Osaka discussions. But this is simply China's transitory ploy to buy time, as it continues to consolidate its global rise to power, in a zero-sum game with the U.S. Beware of letting one matter smokescreen the other.

Toward the end of his news conference, Mr. Trump told a Chinese reporter that China and the U.S. could become "strategic partners who can help each other if the right deal is structured. We can be great for each other. If China opens up it would be tremendous. It is the largest market in the world. Right now China is not open to the United States, but we are open to China. That should have never been allowed to happen."

Unexpectedly, or perhaps remarkably, Donald Trump made a lot of sense for once. Let's hope he continues to tweet this rational reading of China over the rest of his presidency.

This column reported and expanded on a startling international news story about a Chinese government agency covertly running more than 50 clandestine "police service centres" in cities around the world — including three in Toronto, home to Canada's largest Chinese diaspora.

Why are Chinese police operating in Canada, while our own government and security services apparently look the other way?

THE GLOBE AND MAIL, 26 SEPTEMBER 2022

IN CHINA, THE HIGH-PROFILE TV DRAMA *In the Name of the People* has become a smash hit. In that show, Chinese agents enter the U.S. posing as businessmen so they can repatriate a factory manager who had fled abroad with huge ill-gotten wealth.

But a new study by the European non-governmental agency Safeguard Defenders suggests that there might be some truth to the fiction. According to the NGO, the Fuzhou Public Security Bureau has established more than 50 "overseas police service centres" in cities around the world — including three publicly documented ones in Toronto, home to Canada's largest Chinese diaspora.

This is an outrage. Chinese police setting up offices in Canada, then "persuading" alleged criminals to return to the motherland to face "justice" — while our own government and security services apparently choose to look the other way — represents a gross violation of Canada's national sovereignty, international law and the norms of diplomacy. China is extending the grip of its Orwellian police state into this country, with seemingly no worry about being confronted by our own national security agencies.

The RCMP and politicians of all stripes routinely condemn Chinese state harassment of people in Canada, but what action has been taken? There have been no arrests or any expulsion of any Chinese diplomats who might be co-ordinating this kind of thuggery.

Beijing describes these global police outposts as administrative centres to help Chinese nationals renew driver's licences and other domestic banalities back home. But the Safeguard Defenders study found that they also hunt down political dissidents, corrupt officials or rogue Chinese alleged criminals and urge them to return home.

The summary says some of these operatives are given cover by being formally attached to local Chinese Overseas Home Associations (which have themselves largely become co-opted by the Chinese Communist Party's United Front Work operations and run out of China's embassy and consulates).

This bold strategy is consistent with China's propensity for routinely flouting international laws, including those that require any other country's police wishing to gather evidence in Canada to work through the RCMP.

In the case of these "police service centres," Safeguard Defenders reports that agents press their targets to return home, including by offering vague promises of leniency or even urging families back home to encourage them to do so. The officers have taken aim at these alleged (and unproven) criminals by seizing their families' assets, denying children in China access to schools, and terminating family members' employment, all in violation of due process.

In Canada, this has been a reality for years. In 2001, during refugee hearings in Vancouver for Lai Changxing — a businessman wanted by Beijing over accusations of corruption and smuggling — Chinese police admitted to entering Canada using fake documents, and even to spiriting in Mr. Lai's brother in an attempt to convince him to return home. Canadian authorities effectively smiled benignly at this serious breach of criminal and immigration law; Mr. Lai was eventually deported back to China.

Canada is becoming China's chew toy. Consider Beijing's alleged disinformation campaign which helped "unfriendly" Conservative MPs of Chinese ethnicity, including Kenny Chiu, lose their seats in the 2021 federal election.

Ottawa wants Canadian businesses to be able to tap into the world's largest market. But the price of this access appears to be ignoring Beijing's Canadian agenda, from military and industrial espionage to harassing Canadian Uyghurs, Tibetans, Falun Gong practitioners and ethnic Chinese and Taiwanese people who reject Beijing's hectoring that they should be loyal to China instead of to Canada.

Does Canada have no security capabilities on the issue? Our police and security agencies must surely know what is going on, but for some reason prefer to simply curate their information rather than act on it. When asked by *The Globe and Mail* about the police service centres, an RCMP spokesperson said the force would not comment on "uncorroborated media reports or statements." And most of the information we receive about China's illegal and "grey zone" activities in Canada typically comes from the U.S. government and well-funded security and intelligence-focused think tanks in Australia and Europe.

The more we ignore reports of China's growing presence in Canada — including its interference in our electoral process, its potential espionage in our universities and research institutes, and so on — the more emboldened and manipulative Chinese agents become. With no sign that it will be held accountable, China will only increase the size and threat of its operations, because it can.

With its seeming indifference toward China's blatant contempt for our laws and security, Ottawa is playing an extremely dangerous game with Canada's sovereignty.

By 2023 we were well aware of China's interference in Canadian elections and other aspects of our sovereignty — and, equally alarming, the Canadian government's lethargic response to such attacks. This article gave readers some clarity on what was taking place.

What is Ottawa doing to protect Canada's sovereignty against China?

THE GLOBE AND MAIL, 21 FEBRUARY 2023

CANADIANS IN EVERY CORNER OF THIS country need to be alarmed by the latest evidence that China has criminally interfered with, and attempted to influence the results of, Canada's last two federal elections.

But equally concerning is the Canadian government's languid response to these shocking reports — compiled by the Canadian Security Intelligence Service (CSIS), but revealed in *The Globe and Mail* — which detail an extensive scheme meant to corrupt our elections and determine which political party forms Canada's federal government, as well as the kind of power the elected government would be allowed to wield.

Globe journalists viewed secret documents from Canada's most senior security agency alleging that Chinese diplomats in Canada have recruited proxies to smear candidates deemed critical of China, and have funded the campaigns of their rivals, in a program aimed at preventing the Conservative Party from winning elections in 2019 and 2021.

While the blockbuster reporting is startling in its access to credible and top-secret information sources, the fact is that in recent years Canada's leaders have been told numerous times about China's malign influence campaigns operating in this country — and have done little about it.

They were told as recently as Feb. 7, when David Mulroney, Canada's former ambassador in Beijing, testified to the all-party Commons Procedure and House Affairs committee, which is studying alleged foreign election tampering in the campaigns of at least 11 candidates in the 2019 federal election who were both Liberal and Conservative. "Beijing's tools include bribery, disinformation, collusion with criminal gangs and the ever-present threat of hostage-taking. It is increasingly sophisticated in its intimidation of elected officials who dare to speak the truth to Canadians," said Mr. Mulroney. "Beijing's objective is a degree of influence — in our democracy, our economy, our foreign policy and even in daily life in some of our communities — beyond the ambitions of any other country."

I spoke to that same committee about China's massive program of influence-peddling, disinformation and coercion to suppress all voices in Canada critical of Beijing. Last year I sent the same committee a list of 18 reports and journal articles containing authoritative data on how the manipulation works in Canada and abroad.

Given all this evidence, Canadians may well wonder what their government is doing to protect them from China's schemes. Yet no serious action seems to have been taken by Canadian authorities: no court cases or RCMP investigations appear to have been launched, and no diplomats have been ejected. Indeed, the sheer size of Beijing's diplomatic corps here should have long ago raised alarms. China has 146 envoys accredited in Canada, compared to 46 from Japan, 36 from India and 23 for the UK.

We also know the CSIS material has been shared with our Five Eyes global partners and other allied intelligence agencies, as well as among senior government officials; Global News has reported that CSIS briefed Prime Minister Justin Trudeau on interference efforts in the 2019 election. But significantly, it doesn't seem to have been transferred to the RCMP — the organization that would undertake an investigation, lay charges and advise the government about diplomats potentially engaging in these activities, which could be cause to send them back to Beijing.

This past weekend, however, Mr. Trudeau unequivocally stated that "the outcomes of the 2019 and the 2021 elections were determined by Canadians, and Canadians alone, at the voting booth." This was an odd statement to make, however, since Canada is a secret-ballot democracy; we can't tell exactly why people vote the way they vote, and so it seems impossible to actually know if Chinese influence was instrumental in certain political candidates losing their seats.

But we do know that a foreign regime is running a disinformation campaign to try to sabotage Canadian elections. And we know, from the CSIS report, that donors who contribute to Canadian political candidates favoured by Beijing have been quietly and illegally reimbursed for the portion not covered by a federal tax credit.

These sorts of activities, co-ordinated by a hostile power, absolutely should not be tolerated. The RCMP should have long ago been dispatched into action, but we have seen nothing.

The fact that someone inside CSIS was prepared to allow journalists to see classified documents suggests a split inside Ottawa, between a concerned security agency and a political centre that may be too fearful of economic retaliation by China to act. If this interference goes unchecked and there are no criminal or diplomatic consequences, though, it will obviously embolden China to do much more of it.

As General Jennie Carignan becomes the new commander of Canada's Armed Forces, we review the huge logistical and resource challenges facing the overwhelmed military. After decades of underfunding by governments from both main parties, the Forces have nowhere near the equipment or personnel needed to fulfill Canada's NATO commitment. Equally daunting, Canada is woefully incapable of patrolling, let alone defending, the sovereignty of its vast Arctic region.

Canada's new top soldier needs to protect our Arctic from China

OTTAWA CITIZEN, 24 JULY 2024

CANADA'S FRESHLY APPOINTED ARMED FORCES CHIEF, Gen. Jennie Carignan, is starting her new job at a time when the country's vulnerability is alarming.

An urgent issue for Carignan is revisiting how our resource-starved military can address legitimate threats to Canadian sovereignty, starting with China's clear desire to exert control over mineral-rich Arctic regions, much as it has overrun international shipping lanes in the South China Sea.

The federal government's new defence strategy warns that China is already "exploring Arctic waters and the sea floor, probing our infrastructure, and collecting intelligence." It also acknowledges Russia's robust Northern Fleet, with its armada of submarines and two-thirds of Moscow's naval nuclear strike capabilities. It also has the world's largest icebreaker fleet.

China, which calls itself a "near-Arctic state," has two medium-strength icebreakers and a larger, more powerful one under construction.

Russia, which conducted joint military exercises with China last summer off the Alaskan coast, continues building more northern military bases. Moscow is currently asking the United Nations to extend its claim to the Arctic seabed and move its territorial claim right up to Canada's 200-mile economic zone.

When Moscow maintains a strong Arctic posture, Beijing benefits. And with Russian support, we should view a Chinese presence on Canada's borders as inevitable.

Canada's defence strategy, meantime, responds by calling for a network of northern operational support hubs, a fleet of early warning aircraft, underwater and coastal sensors, a high Arctic satellite station, and acquiring "up to" 12 under-ice submarines "to ensure our military has the tools to assert our sovereignty and protect Canada's interests."

However, there is no plan in place to fund these aspirations. Ottawa says the next defence funding announcements will occur four years from now, with a "promise" of implementation by 2032.

Canada's tattered credibility in terms of paying its promised share of defence costs had eyes rolling at the recent NATO summit, where scorn from our allies prompted vague Canadian promises of submarine purchases and other procurements.

Miserly defence spending has long defined federal governments, both Liberal and Conservative. Rather than point fingers, Canadians need to realize that these decisions by politicians really just reflect the tolerances, or desires, of voters.

As for our traditionally protective southern neighbour, regardless of how the U.S. political landscape plays out after Joe Biden's withdrawal from this fall's election, the days of America covering for Canada are gone. Republican policy prioritizing U.S. isolationism over international alliances reflects the sentiments of millions of Americans. The U.S. military presence around the world will henceforth be based on the costs — and benefits — to America.

So when China or Russia encroach on Arctic regions that Canada has always claimed as sovereign territory — but where we have no physical presence — it is folly to expect Donald Trump to rescue us.

If, or when, Washington slashes its funding — which presently accounts for 68 per cent of NATO's budget — it is plausible that Canada will not help European allies cover the shortfall.

Canada could begin salvaging its reputation as a responsible ally if we were seen as legitimately trying to make strenuous efforts to defend our sovereignty with advanced technologies and a highly skilled military. To that end, Gen. Carignan should essentially put Canada on a war footing by taking prominent measures to spotlight and confront our crises of recruitment shortfalls and chronic procurement delays.

Canada must show the world, including our allies, that we have the gumption to defend our borders by being militarily present in the North. We must equip ourselves to take action to counter aggressive Chinese expansionism and prevent Beijing and its subordinate partner, Russia, from controlling crucial shipping routes or gaining access to Canadian natural resources, critical minerals and energy sources.

This is not being hawkish, it's being realistic. The alternative is clear. If we continue to be absent in the Arctic, we will lose it.

Ottawa is between a rock and a hard place. With Donald Trump looking to plunder Canada's industrial base using the weapon of tariffs, companies and governments are racing to find new trading partners so as to minimize our reliance on selling exports to America. An obvious possibility would be to try and cut a trade treaty with China, given its massive industrial and consumer market. But that is the last thing Canada should do.

As Canada scrambles for options, beware the temptation of China

THE GLOBE AND MAIL, 6 FEBRUARY 2025

DONALD TRUMP'S WRECKING-BALL ADMINISTRATION IS JUST weeks into a four-year term, and as he makes his moves to decimate Canada's economy and sovereignty, intelligent minds in both countries worry that his irrational trade war will push Canada into the arms of Beijing.

It is naïve to think Mr. Trump's end game is fentanyl and immigrants. Tariffs are just the beginning, and Canadians should anticipate culture-changing ultimatums that go beyond tripling our defence spending or scrapping dairy-industry supply management. We should expect demands like abandoning content guidelines for U.S.-based social-media companies operating in Canada, and cancelling environmental or Indigenous rights barriers for U.S. mining operations in our North. And how about a joint currency, or letting U.S. health conglomerates provide for-profit medical services in Canada? As the world is witnessing with Mr. Trump, nothing is beyond consideration.

Canadian efforts to improve productivity or reduce interprovincial trade barriers won't offset this massive assault. The demise of our auto and steel sectors, and the loss of some businesses to U.S. locations, will result in mass unemployment and governments struggling to sustain services. Anxious to avoid a deep recession, governments are scrambling to find new markets and trading partners.

This is where China will come in, dangling its version of a lifeline: Let's hit the reset button, put aside our past differences and generate economic benefits for all. Beijing knows Canada will be desperate for access to China's vast market and will require our compliance with Chinese conditions — ones that will be as onerous as anything Mr. Trump hopes to extract from us.

Beijing has its own "Make China Great Again" agenda, expanding its grip throughout the world. Raising its involvement in Canada will bring China's agenda to Mr. Trump's doorstep.

Canada's pro-China business faction will push Ottawa to engage with China in areas that do not threaten our national security; let the two Michaels nightmare be bygones, and move on. As former MP Wai Young (vying to become the Conservative candidate in the Steveston-Richmond East riding in B.C.) avers, the Hogue Commission's report shows "there was no real foreign interference" — an interpretation not shared by most informed observers of China's massive Canadian operations.

China wants access to our resources, including the same critical minerals the Trumpists crave, and access to our Arctic for not just economic reasons but for geostrategic domination. Canada needs to remember its history here: There were legitimate security reasons for why Ottawa banned Huawei and Nuctech from the Canadian market, squelched the sale of Aecon construction to a Chinese company and turned down Shandong Gold's attempt to buy a money-losing mine in a strategic location in our far North.

The latest concern is that Chinese-manufactured TP-Link routers, which enable Wi-Fi in many Canadian homes and businesses, have the potential to be used in cyberattacks by China. Surrendering an embedded presence within our data infrastructure would be a huge liability in any future hybrid warfare, should Canada find itself on the U.S. side in a conflict over, say, the South China Sea or Korea or Taiwan.

Beijing's demands will be political as well as economic. For example, China may expect Canada to formally terminate its principled position against Beijing's policies of genocide against Uyghurs and other minorities, its gross violations of international law, its autocratic hostility toward democracy or its betrayal of Hong Kong, including bounties on pro-democracy advocates here in Canada.

We have been down this road before. In 1994, while trying to broaden our economy away from U.S. dependence, prime minister Jean Chrétien led a 300-member "Team Canada" trade mission to China. Besides drumming up new business, Mr. Chrétien believed that getting China more immersed in international commerce could eventually lead Beijing to adopt the rule of law and advance human rights. Thirty years later, Canada's trade with China remains at a three-to-one imbalance, Beijing still bans foreign companies from key sectors of its economy, and it is more authoritarian than ever.

In terms of relieving our trade dependence by achieving a fair relationship with China, we couldn't achieve it when Canada was in a relatively sound situation, and it's even less likely to happen in our current state of economic vulnerability.

As Canada sits pinched between a rock and a hard place, the next federal government faces a conundrum. Pursuing closer ties to China could boost our economic prospects but would also undercut a key goal of Mr. Trump's: to constrain China's global expansion. In terms of our relations with the new White House regime, that would put Canada in an even more unfavourable light than we are in now.

As Donald Trump abuses and abandons America's traditional allies — evidently eyeing a new world order where Washington, Beijing and Moscow carve out their respective zones of influence — this piece cuts to the president's apparent end game for Canada: crippling it economically in order to force it to become a compliant U.S. territory, helpless to stop the pillaging of our sovereign lands and the riches of our natural resources.

Donald Trump has extreme designs on Canada: Here is what he really wants

TORONTO STAR, 6 MARCH 2025

THE TARIFFS HAVE ARRIVED — AND BEEN quickly paused — yet a potential trade war and retaliatory measures still hang over relations between Canada and the United States.

U.S. President Donald Trump has extreme designs on Canada. He also has a playbook: Trigger a crisis with ultimatums too vague to be met, negotiate with conditions that would be crippling, then "settle" for the actual goals: fresh water, minerals, manufacturing jobs.

Deciphering months of his rhetoric, expect demands like unfettered economic participation (U.S. airlines flying our domestic routes?); DOGE-like demolition of food supply management; selling private

American health care Canada-wide; U.S. banks in every town (one of his obsessions).

As for grabbing natural resources, think Ukraine. Because wealthier, more populous America has borne most of the cost of North American defence, Trump will demand massive retro-compensation in return for lifting devastating tariffs. No more neighbourhood discount on mutual security, or sharing U.S. intelligence through the Five Eyes alliance.

As those "51st-state" taunts purposely imply, a sinister threat menaces our political, cultural and economic autonomy. Trump has little interest in sovereign borders or international law, and as the world abruptly careens with startling speed toward great-power imperialism, he is quickly realigning with Moscow and Beijing to revive colonial-like control over nations too weak to repel well-armed autocrats.

Canada isn't the only hostage in this maze of greed, but we're fully exposed in the very front row for Donald Trump's line of fire.

This is a legitimately existential moment when Canadians must unite, and the country must have determined leadership — in Ottawa and in every provincial capital — that discards partisan division and regionalism in favour of collaboration and the poise to identify all sensible measures required to confront the challenges we face.

In the English-language Liberal leadership debate, Mark Carney asserted that the U.S. represents a threat to Canadian sovereignty over the Arctic, warning that Canada's Arctic is under threat, not just from Russia and China, but "potential U.S. incursions."

Is the future of global politics one of Trump collaborating with Vladimir Putin and Xi Jinping in a grand bargain to recast geopolitical power into a mould that benefits Russian oligarchs, American high-tech billionaires and the Chinese communists?

It is not only possible but probable that they would adopt a normality of looting precious minerals wherever they exist, including in Canada's Arctic. It has echoes of 19th-century powers carving up of Africa, Asia and Latin America for minerals and agricultural commodities exploitation.

Trump has obviously been candid in voicing his desire to seize strategic control of Greenland. Canada's north is a logical next step.

The world order is being vandalized in a way that nobody alive has ever seen. Consider China's blatant naval push into international waters of the South China Sea and Taiwan Strait toward Australia; Russia's expansion into Ukraine and presumably beyond; and Trump's threatened economic coercion over Canada, Britain and the EU.

Nearly a century after global disruption was engendered by 1930s Germany, we again see urgently convened international gatherings characterized by weak gestures of appeasement based on delusionary hopes that, if we make gestures to stem an alleged flood of opioids and undocumented migrants, Trump will back off.

Western democracies are grappling to maintain a shared but faltering doctrine of freedoms and justice. Unfortunately some stymied leaders recall Neville Chamberlain, who went to Munich to placate Hitler. Today, western leaders fly to Washington or Mar-a-Lago. Chamberlain returned to the U.K. famously proclaiming, "Peace in our time!"

Eleven months later, the Second World War began.

For the past 80 years a critical mass of allied nations has steadied international economics and entrenched principles like basic human rights and the integrity of sovereign borders. Today that same community — just six weeks after Trump's inauguration — finds itself in threatening chaos with few palatable solutions at hand.

After Canada used tariffs to shield its auto industry from China's heavily subsidized EVs, Beijing retaliated with crippling tariffs on Canadian agricultural commodities. Then, taking malevolence to new heights, Beijing ordered the execution of four Canadians held in Chinese prisons for drugs offences. When Ottawa requested some semblance of mercy, Chinese officials scoffed.

China weaponizes death penalty as relations with Canada deteriorate

TORONTO STAR, 22 MARCH 2025

CHINA'S EXECUTION OF FOUR CANADIANS IS APPALLING NOT just for the loss of life, but how state-ordered killings can be used as a weapon to send menacing diplomatic messages.

Coming at a time when Beijing is unleashing harsh tariffs intended to damage Canada's economic security, these executions will only further diminish Canada-China relations.

Both Foreign Affairs Minister Mélanie Joly and former prime minister Justin Trudeau had asked China for leniency toward the Canadians — dual citizens who faced drug-related criminal charges.

In China the judiciary is not independent, it is politically controlled. Convictions are reviewed by the Communist Party's Political and Legal

Affairs Commissions and death sentences are automatically subject to reconsideration by the Supreme Court in Beijing.

In other words, it is within the authority of our prime minister's senior level Chinese interlocutors to order clemency. One word from Xi Jinping would have avoided the deaths of the Canadians, whose names have not been released by the Chinese or Canadian governments.

In China, crimes punishable by death include non-violent offences like drug possession and use or financial fraud. The capital punishment death toll is a state secret, though it is thought China executes more prisoners than all other countries combined.

Currently around 100 Canadians are in Chinese prisons, many on drugs charges. Under China's legal process, once a case gets into the courtroom, the accused has little opportunity to mount a defence and the rules of evidence fall short of international standards.

A particularly disturbing aspect of these latest killings is the spectre of why they were ordered. Executing four Canadians, while other foreign nationals in Chinese judicial limbo avoid the death penalty, sends a horrifying signal that appears linked to Canada's compliance with Donald Trump's demands to bar Chinese EVs from North America.

Canada imposed a 100 per cent tariff on Chinese EVs because Ottawa claimed they are being sold below the cost of production, an unfair tactic that would devastate Canadian automakers. (Canada applied a 25-per-cent levy on Chinese steel and aluminum for the same reason. Beijing's response was a 100-per-cent tariff on Canadian canola oil, oil cakes and pea imports, as well as a 25-per-cent duty on Canadian pork and aquatic products. That's $3.7-billion worth of economic penalties.)

This, compounded by the Trump administration's own economic aggression, puts immense pressure on Ottawa to find a resolution with China on the EVs in order to save the livelihoods of Canadian farmers and fishers.

But besides the economic casualties caused by dumping underpriced cars into Canada, the technology-laced Chinese EVs are also security threats, rolling spy stations whose sensors constantly collect information about their drivers and critical infrastructure everywhere the car goes. (In China, Teslas are banned from sensitive areas for exactly this reason.)

In a case of extreme diplomatic tensions, Beijing could order manufacturers to use software updates that disable thousands of EVs across Canada. So, from China's geostrategic standpoint, the 100-per-cent tariff on EVs is about much more than losing a car sales market in Canada.

While China's Communist leadership will undoubtedly continue employing whatever means available to leverage Foreign Minister Joly and Prime Minister Mark Carney into reversing the EV tariffs, the question is, will there be more executions of Canadians in China as a preposterously gruesome pressure tactic.

The earnest entreaties by Trudeau and Joly that mercy be shown to the Canadians were not just ignored but scorned by China, which immediately ordered their execution in response. Canada is seen as weaker than other Western nations and thus open to being perversely coerced in this repugnant manner.

As Ottawa looks to strengthen relations on all levels with Europe, Japan, South Korea and other Indo-Pacific democracies, China and Trump appear to be in concert tightening the screws on a country whose culture they evidently loathe but whose assets they both covet.

Xi Jinping's fundamental vision is for China to become the world's unrivalled and dominant superpower by 2050. Achieving this requires the demise of U.S. global power and of bodies like NATO and the UN. Donald Trump's apparent pursuit of American isolationism should be very helpful to fulfilling Xi's plan.

Donald Trump is helping Xi Jinping achieve his grand vision for China

THE GLOBE AND MAIL, 24 MARCH 2025

IT'S HARD TO REMEMBER, AMIDST ALL the news out of Washington, that China was unhappy when Donald Trump won November's U.S. election.

The economic warfare of his first presidency had not been forgotten in Beijing — and after inauguration day, things only got worse. Mr. Trump appointed China hawk Marco Rubio as Secretary of State, clamped down on Chinese espionage, restricted exports of U.S. chips essential to China's tech sector, and imposed restrictions on Chinese ownership of American farmland, resources, tech companies, ports and other infrastructure. Now, the President reportedly wants Chinese companies to sell any holdings deemed threatening to America's security.

So why has the Chinese government's response been relatively muted?

In 2012, Xi Jinping declared his "Chinese Dream": a foreign-policy vision "realizing the great renewal of the Chinese nation is the greatest dream for the Chinese nation in modern history." By 2050, China would dominate the world through a framework of international relations that Mr. Xi dubs "the community of common destiny for mankind."

But achieving such a tectonic shift would require the U.S. to cease being the guardian of world democracies and of organizations like NATO, the United Nations and the World Trade Organization, which promote justice and global prosperity.

Well, Mr. Trump's aggressive abandonment of America's longtime alliances is doing just that. And regardless of tariffs and whatever becomes of MAGA plans for Panama, Gaza, Greenland or Canada, his administration's abandonment of nearly all soft-power initiatives – from defunding Radio Free Asia to freezing foreign aid – leaves a vacuum that China's disinformation media ecosystem and Belt and Road initiative will quickly fill.

Perhaps that is why Beijing has taken a relatively measured, even flattering, tone to Washington's activities. Beijing has sought a "win-win solution" for trade tensions, and Chinese state-run media outlets have celebrated Mr. Trump's funding cuts for Voice of America. Mr. Xi was even invited to Mr. Trump's inauguration. It's only in the last month, amid tariffs and retaliation, that China's rhetoric has toughened.

And why not? Mr. Trump's mercenary "America First" doctrine – abandoning the rest of the world to other powers' "spheres of influence," which will lead millions to economic desperation and disease – is a gift to Mr. Xi. The era of American betrayal, contrasted by the smiling face of Beijing's blandishments, will tip the geostrategic balance in the Chinese leader's favour.

Canada, meanwhile, has suddenly realized how much our complacent dependency on the U.S. as a defence backstop and an easy market for exports has weakened our country. We virtuously declined to develop nuclear weapons, because the U.S. had them. We were thrifty in our military spending, knowing Washington would pick up the slack. The payoff for this cleverness: our productivity innovation and per-capita income stagnated.

Today, Mr. Trump's "Golden Dome" seabed-to-space missile defence shield plan no longer includes Canada's north. And as America moves from protector to predator, Ottawa must seriously consider cancelling our much-needed order of Lockheed Martin F-35 fighter jets, because we can't risk exposing our security to U.S.-controlled technologies.

Canada can avoid becoming a U.S. vassal by establishing balanced, strategic relations with powers to our east, west and north, but that will require a vision and determination that has been sorely lacking in our leaders. What we need is a modern-day Winston Churchill, but as the 7th-century Chinese poet Chen Zi'ang lamented when the Tang Dynasty was in a similar existential crisis, "The greats of the past are nowhere to be seen, and there doesn't appear to be any of their ilk coming to the fore."

Canada cannot count on Europe or the Indo-Pacific to significantly support our defence against potential threats from China, Russia – or the U.S. There will be no payback for our past support of Ukraine, Taiwan, South Korea, Japan – that was never a two-way street.

As we move forward into uncharted waters, the only country that will defend Canada from predatory expansionists is Canada itself. The challenge is to proceed with dignity, courage and clarity of purpose.

All of this feeds into Xi Jinping's Chinese Dream, which would fulfill his historic ambition to restore China to imperial domination of "all under heaven" as the Chinese emperors of ancient times.

Mr. Xi has evoked Mao Zedong in his confidence that "the east wind" will prevail over the West. In this setting, the folly of MAGA is fast-tracking the shift in the weather patterns.

Even when Mr. Trump is gone, Canada will have to rise to even greater challenges – and we can.

In this post-international-rules-based era, decades of feeble foreign and defence policies have left Canada vulnerable to expansionist predators like Xi Jinping and now Donald Trump who prey on the weak. No longer complacent, Ottawa works with urgency to cultivate new trade and foreign policy alliances, and re-energize some old ones.

Canada in trade wars with the superpowers – with no room for error

TORONTO STAR, 7 APRIL 2025

THE ACHE OF DONALD TRUMP'S LIBERATION DAY noir will go beyond disaster for thousands of Canadians who lose their jobs and see their savings debased by stagflation and battered markets. There will also be historic political implications for whoever forms Canada's next government.

While we were "spared" the heavier blows that Trump placed on many other countries, Canadian households very much face a painful future of reduced incomes, diminished nest eggs and higher living costs.

Canada is entering its greatest existential upheaval since Confederation. Besides Trump duties that will make Canadian autos, steel and aluminum less affordable to U.S. customers, China has slapped exorbitant tariffs on Canadian canola, seafood and pork exports that will punish farming and commercial fishing families.

The fitful week ended with China answering Trump's aggression by announcing its own anti-U.S. tariffs, causing the kind of uncertainty that sends financial markets toward meltdown.

As Trump's pathological behaviour puts global recession on the table and provides an opening for China to play its own agenda, trade-dependent nations like Canada will find it prohibitively difficult to sustain their economies by selling exports.

Canadians will demand Ottawa grab any measure it can to relieve the pain. This is where poise and critical judgment must be paramount.

Amidst the chaos, China has already indicated it is open to new trade talks with Canada. All we need to do is make concessions, like removing Canada's 100-per-cent tariff on massively subsidized electric vehicles that China wants to dump here, idling our auto industry and vaporizing thousands of jobs. (China has spent $230-billion USD helping state-controlled industries developing its EV industry. It has double the production capacity its domestic market needs and plans to secure global domination.)

Strong-armed by Beijing and hectored by U.S. ideologues renegotiating CUSMA, Canadian officials will be disadvantaged — especially now that protections like the WTO or "legally binding treaties" are worthless. There will be no David and Goliath outcome, no principles of reciprocal fairness, no goodwill toward Canada.

Trump tactics like demanding that NATO nations hike military spending to 5 per cent of GDP not only benefit American defence contractors but present an impossible task for Canada as it struggles to support its workers and restructure its economy. That then becomes a rationale for further penalties like closing off U.S. markets, imposing secondary tariffs, and of course playing the Trump card for our resources and Arctic sovereignty.

CANADA'S SOVEREIGNTY VS CHINA AND TRUMP

Stalked by China, estranged from our erstwhile U.S. partner, and an ocean away from European allies, Canada must tread carefully and strategically as it reorganizes relationships and navigates the shoals of the new age. Trump is already promising further kamikaze tariffs if we jointly retaliate with Europe. Beijing will use similar threats if Ottawa moves to protect Canadian sovereignty by countering Chinese espionage, influence, interference, bribery and intimidation operations here.

Most economists outside of the acerbic MAGA cult know that Trump's senseless tariffs will damage the U.S. economy, and while the president is erratic in most respects, one thing we can safely predict is that any spike in unemployment or crashing of markets will not be his fault.

Global economic carnage is being triggered by Trump's greed to have it all, which itself is based on carefully concocted propaganda that America has been "looted, pillaged, raped and plundered" by duplicitous allies that past U.S. administrations have been stupidly subsidizing. Canada evidently tops the list of freeloaders.

As the havoc of Liberation Day metastasizes, any harms to U.S. prosperity will be blamed on Canada and Europe, provoking Trump to deliriously unleash further punishments. Beijing, meanwhile, is biding its time.

Between studying the content patterns of China's state-controlled news media, and deciphering the official-speak of Communist Party announcements, Burton picks up on a major realignment taking place: the regime is taking steps to clip the wings of China's self-styled dictator.

New evidence indicates China's Communist Party is reining in strongman Xi Jinping

TORONTO STAR, 7 JULY 2025

THERE ARE NEW SIGNS THAT CHINA'S Communist apparatus is dismantling Xi Jinping's dictatorship-like rule, continuing a sense of turmoil within the Communist Party of China (CPC) ever since Xi disappeared from public view for two weeks this spring for reasons never explained.

This week, evidence of a power "correction" went public as CPC officials rescinded Xi's absolute control over both domestic and foreign policy, announcing new rules to "standardize the establishment, responsibilities and operations of the central committee's decision-making, deliberative and co-ordinating institutions."

Translating that bafflegab: General Secretary Xi Jinping is no longer China's unchallenged strongman leader, no longer the "pilot at the helm" who entrenched one-man power on the claim that it was a necessity for the country.

If Xi is being sidelined, any consequent chaos in Beijing presents a deep concern for a world already grappling to maintain balance against crises relentlessly choreographed by Donald Trump. Given its massive global influence, volatility within China raises instant questions about how its official attitudes could change. As it is, Taiwan's military already predicts Xi could launch an invasion by 2027, a view shared in the Pentagon.

Xi's grip on power has been buttressed by his emperor-like charisma as supreme leader. But while the outside world sees China through a global lens, Xi's domestic problems stem from disastrous economic and foreign policies that hobbled the economy, leaving local governments in debt and real estate values plunging.

As a Rand Corporation summary puts it, "Consumer confidence is poor. External demand is a brittle support beam, as Western governments consider protectionist measures. China's GDP is no longer catching up to the United States."

While China's high tech may be soaring, public confidence is low because of Xi's repressive policies and plummeting relations with the West. There are no mechanisms to push him into retirement, however there are powerful rivals within the party — and a military that resents 10 years of politically motivated corruption purges.

In consolidating power, Xi removed any Party voices allied to his predecessors, then repealed China's two-term limit on the presidency. Of 2,964 delegates at the National People's Congress, just two voted against that change, and three abstained. But few outside of Xi and his sycophants likely supported the change — and we might now be seeing their return to power.

The past two months of CPC media propaganda has shown a sharp drop in Xi's visibility, with many appearances purely ceremonial or even recycled. A June 10 broadcast about a community centre visit actually used footage from 2018.

Xi's conspicuous absence from leadership functions, combined with the disappearance of laudatory titles like "the people's leader," suggest more of a figurehead than hands-on leader. Newscasts no longer show Xi directing Politburo sessions, with members dutifully taking notes. Instead, Premier Li Qiang and Political Consultative Conference Chair Wang Huning are now seen chairing key meetings.

On June 13, the evolution became apparent at a symposium for the 120th anniversary of the birth of Chen Yun, a senior leader who died in 1995. In his speech, Xi was compelled to praise Chen's economic work and his function within the "leadership collectives" of Mao and Deng — an obvious reference to the merits of shared leadership. Unusually, the broadcast showed no applause for Xi's address.

But even as it adjusts China's leadership mechanism and prepares for what comes next, the party's traditional claim to unquestioned rule is vulnerable. After a generation of growing affluence and lifestyle security, citizens expect more than their parents did. If the CPC cannot deliver economic growth and political stability, chaos may follow.

Hopefully any change will lead to China becoming a responsible global stakeholder, though the prevailing political trends are away from liberal democracy. Whoever follows Xi, whenever that happens, it could be even worse.

Dilemma / (d'leme) / n. — A situation in which a choice has to be made between two equally undesirable alternatives; a difficult situation.

By summer 2025, White House disdain for Canada was increasingly blunt. Officials' comments were becoming taunts, Canada was slapped with steeper tariffs than most allies, and Trump administration officials were promising the Canada-US-Mexico trade agreement would be renegotiated "to protect American jobs". It's little wonder Ottawa was turning its attention to possible new trading partners.

Is China a better trading partner than Trump's America?

THE GLOBE AND MAIL, 1 AUGUST 2025

THERE ARE INCREASING SIGNS THAT MARK Carney's cabinet, which is anxiously trying to mend our crumbling alliance with the United States, is quietly pursuing a major policy shift in Canada's relations with China.

Foreign Minister Anita Anand reinforced the notion after meeting with her Asian counterparts in Malaysia in early July. "It is important for us to revisit our policy — not only in the Indo-Pacific but generally speaking — to ensure that we are focusing not only on the values that we have historically adhered to," she said.

"Foreign policy is an extension of domestic interest and particularly domestic economic interests," she added. "This is a time when the global economy is under stress."

In the 35 years since Chinese tanks crushed the 1989 Tiananmen Square democracy demonstrations — killing some 4,000 citizens in Beijing alone, mostly young, politically idealistic students — the discussion within Canada has become whether we should forget such history and focus on growing trade with superpower China on its terms, downplaying concerns over its threat to Canada's security, sovereignty and democratic values that support rules-based international order.

As federal officials engage in bare-knuckle tariff talks with U.S. negotiators, Canada obviously needs to restructure its trade and security partnerships to build a buffer from Donald Trump, who is manipulating commercial gravity to pull industries to relocate to the States. One aim is to reduce Canada to the status of a toothless neighbour forced to grant more U.S. access to, say, our fresh water and critical minerals.

Watching this unfold, China is ramping up specious propaganda that it respects fair trade through the World Trade Organization, supports measures that mitigate climate change, and provides loans and aid to developing countries through its Belt and Road program and its Asian Infrastructure Investment Bank. The message is clear: China is a better and more ethical partner for Canada than Trumpian America.

In June, Mr. Carney and Chinese Premier Li Qiang agreed to "regularize communications" between the countries and revive the moribund Canada-China Joint Economic and Trade Commission, which was created when Stephen Harper was Canada's prime minister.

Canada wants China to lift its punishing tariffs on Canadian agricultural and seafood products, which were imposed last fall in response to Canada's 100-per-cent tariff on imported Chinese EVs. If it becomes obvious that Mr. Trump's abrogation of the 1965 Canada-U.S. Auto

Pact is inevitable, Ottawa may decide to let China's state-subsidized, inexpensive spy machines on wheels flood our market and devastate Canada's auto industry.

China and the U.S. appear to be equally treacherous options for Canada, and for many countries.

When Australian Prime Minister Anthony Albanese met recently in Beijing with Xi Jinping, the Chinese Leader made the standard comment that Western nations dealing with China should "seek common ground while setting aside differences." Mr. Albanese actually concurred, saying, "That approach has indeed produced very positive benefits for both Australia and for China."

Unfortunately, the "differences" that Mr. Xi talks about result in harms to Canada, not China. For Ottawa, the price of enhanced trade would be dear: Let China mine critical minerals in Canada's North, give open access to Canadian high tech and dual-use military technologies, abandon implementing a foreign influence transparency registry, accept China's incursions in the Canadian Arctic, and cease Canada's modest freedom of navigation exercises in the South China Sea and Taiwan Strait. And those are just for starters.

The Trump administration likewise has a deep agenda and savours capitulation. Mr. Trump wants Canada to beg to become the 51st state, extending U.S. territory all the way to Greenland. Is it even possible to negotiate an economic and defence deal with Washington, salvaging some semblance of benefit to Canada, while paying no mind to Mr. Trump's threats to devastate Canada's economy?

Caught in a bind between superpowers, it will not likely be long before Mr. Carney follows Mr. Albanese to Beijing. He has been to China and met Mr. Xi before. But getting in bed with the Communist Party of China could make a bad situation for Canada irreversibly worse.

Hope for the future

MY HECTIC GETAWAY FROM SHANGHAI AIRPORT in 2018 was the last time I've set foot in China. Given the circumstances, it obviously made sense to delay any return until we could determine what concerns the regime has about me, and how they could be resolved without involving arrest or harassment.

In December 2024 my absence was no longer self-imposed when I along with 19 other individuals and two Canadian organizations were banned from entering China. I was on the list because I had acted as an advisor for a Canada-based human rights group, the Uyghur Rights Advocacy Project (although I qualified to make the list twice due to my similar association with the Canada Tibet Committee).

This came days after Canada had announced sanctions against eight Chinese government officials it said were involved in human rights violations against ethnic and religious minorities in Xinjiang and Tibet, as well as against practitioners of Falun Gong.

After our banishment was posted on a government website, the Chinese Communist Party-controlled newspaper the *Global Times* reported that we were exiled for offences that included "spreading disinformation" about human rights violations in China's Xinjiang Uyghur Autonomous Region and in Tibet. (PRC official propaganda has recently started to refer to Tibet by its name in romanized Chinese, which is "xizang", meaning literally "western treasury." It is politically motivated subterfuge to downplay that Tibet has been the ancestral lands of Tibetans since long before the Han Chinese invaded the territory).

The Chinese official statement reads, "Canada's actions are an attempt to use human rights issues in Xinjiang and Xizang to enhance its international presence and strengthen its influence in global diplomacy and ideological discourse."

So, unlike my sanctioning by Russia in 2022, China did not ban me because of what I have published in newspapers. It was a response to Canada's China policy in general.

―――

When I began placing opinion pieces in Canadian newspapers nearly 20 years ago, many Canadians were confident that China could become a responsible stakeholder in world affairs. Canada under Justin Trudeau came close to collaborating with China in international affairs including transnational crime, even considering an extradition treaty. We also came close to integrating our economies through a free trade deal.

But, as the commentary articles recount, as China became more powerful economically, it began posing a hostile geostrategic threat to the international rules based order.

China's current leadership sees Donald Trump as fulfilling Xi Jinping's prediction that the United States is a power in decline, that the vacuum created by American nationalism will be filled by China, and that Xi's "Community of the Common Destiny of Mankind" will become the future global order. China thus assumes what Mr. Xi considers its rightful role as the dominant global civilization, with Chinese even displacing English as the world's foremost common language.

Under Xi's vision, Canadians would realize that a political system based on China's authoritarian model, and on its superior civilization informed by Confucianism, is Canada's best option for political, economic and social development. Canada would become a subsidiary economy to China's centre of global industrial production and infrastructure.

But there are other, less oppressive possible futures.

Some China watchers see Xi's domestic and international ideology eventually being rejected by the Chinese people. They question the very sustainability of his Leninist model, which favours unquestioned state domination and purges non-regime actors like Alibaba founder Jack Ma or others who develop power bases that could challenge Beijing's influence.

In China there is the expression *wu ji bi fan*, meaning that "when things go to extremes they must turn back." The pendulum of history may turn back to the ideals of liberal democracy.

It is plausible that a demise of American world dominance would give way to the creation of a renewed global order where China plays a productive role in enabling sovereign states to engage in free and fair trade, but where the United Nations and other organizations that protect sovereign nations would be reinvigorated.

The work that I was doing in the 1980s and '90s, before Xi came to power, was to try and provide the Chinese government with information about how it might transition to a governance system based on rule of law. In such a scenario, the kinds of political institutions defined in the UN charter — particularly the International Covenant on Civil and Political Rights, which China signed in 1998 and but never ratified — could become relevant to China's political development.

A politically renewed China could lead the way against the current trend where values and organizations like the UN and WTO are being debased. Even before Trump came along, they were already showing signs of fraying. The ideals of human rights and citizenship, and of equality of all the humans on the planet, were deteriorating.

So, a hopeful scenario for the future could actually emerge from the assault on our institutions by the Trumpist United States. It would be a renaissance of democracy in which popular global forces unify to counterbalance the wealth and power of global elites with reinvigorated political and multilateral institutions that are based in the inherent equal rights of free citizens.

Despite all the setbacks and unfulfilled promises of my more than half a century of intense engagement with China, I remain optimistic that its best days are still ahead.

Index

Africa, 110, 201, 220
"America First", 108, 176, 225
Americans, 146, 214
Amnesty International, 66, 161
Analects of Confucius, 9–10
Anchorage, 166
Arctic regions, 212–14
Asia Infrastructure Investment Bank, 194
Asia Pacific Economic Cooperation Summit, 44–7
Asia, 157, 201, 220
Aung San Suu Kyi, 32
Australia, 20, 27, 75, 99, 114–16, 207
  implemented China-proactive policies, 38
  investigation COVID-19 pandemic, 190
  refusal to One Belt One Road, 107
Australia-China Free Trade Agreement (2014), 115
Austria, 53

Baird, John, 33–4, 37, 39, 48–50
Bangladesh, 185
Barton, Dominic, 161
Beijing Olympics (2008), 45
Bell, 172, 175
Biden, Joe, 123–5, 164, 213–14
  administration, 114, 115, 166
Big Circle Boys, 34
"Bilateral Dialogues", 14
Bill C-267, 97
Bill C-282, 125
Bill C-70, 132, 134
Bloc Québécois, 26
Bo Xilai, 106

Brady, Anne-Marie, 177
Britain, 20, 49, 107, 185
  declared war with China, 86
  relations with China, 64–7
British Columbia, 233
British India, 85
Brock University, 3
Brontë, Emily, 134
Burma, 32

Calgary, 112
California, 100
Canada's Asia-Pacific Foundation, 76
Canadian Communist Party, 12
Canadian International Council, 161
Canadian International Development Agency, 102, 200
Canadian Security Intelligence Service (CSIS), 119, 127, 154, 179–81, 209, 211
  RCMP and, 137, 150
Canadian Uyghurs, 119, 207
Canadians, 6, 17, 43, 83, 163–4
  concerns about human rights, 78, 81, 93–4, 104
  death in Chinese prisons, 221–3
  detention in China, 141–3
  Magnitsky Act impacts on, 97
  opposed free trade with China, 76
  plans for evacuating from Wuhan, 185–7
  research assistance by Chinese, 122
  See also Hong Kong
Carignan, Jennie, 212, 214s
Carney, Mark, 219, 223, 233, 235
Castro, Fidel, 65

Chamberlain, Neville, 220
Champagne, François-Philippe, 160, 186
Charter of Rights and Freedoms for
    Canadians, 65
Chen Yun, 232
Chen Zi'ang, 226
China Daily (newspaper), 50, 93, 115
China Pictorial (magazine), 7, 8
China Reconstructs (magazine), 7
China-Canada Foreign Ministers
    Dialogue, 91
Chinese Academy of Social Sciences
    (CASS), 12
Chinese Buddhist Philosophy, 8
Chinese Canadians, 125
Chinese Communist Party (CCP), 18,
    38, 39–40, 161, 230, 232
    actions on population growth, 69
    challenge posed by, 166
    COVID-19 epidemic coverup, 192
    historical reluctance moments, 189–90
    Party Committee in Huawei, 173
    policies, 6, 202–3
    public demonstrations against, 129
    true nature of, 167
    Xi Jinping's emergence as General
        Secretary of, 234
Chinese EVs, 223–4
Chinese Exclusion Act (1923), 133
Chinese Literature (magazine), 7
Chinese National Offshore Oil Corp.,
    41–2, 65, 76
Chinese Overseas Home Associations, 206
Chinese People's Political Consultative
    Conference (CPPCC), 53, 121
Choi, Jonathan Koon-Shum, 121
Chrétien, Jean, 13, 26, 65–6, 82, 203
    "Team Canada" trade missions, 103,
        217

CIDA, 15
Communications Security Establishment
    (CSE), 127, 179, 180–1
Communist Politburo, 105
Confucianism, 3, 8, 239
Cong Peiwu, 160–1
coronavirus
    outbreak, 185–7, 191–4
COVID-19, 124, 130–1, 161
    mismanagement of, 190
    See also Wuhan
CPC. *See* Chinese Communist Party (CCP)
CPTPP, 193
CRTC, 12
CSIS. *See* Canadian Security Intelligence
    Service (CSIS)
Cultural Revolution (1966-76), 3, 8, 18,
    49, 106, 200–1
CUSMA, 228
Cyrillic, 10–11

Dandong, 141–2, 144
de Montigny, Yves, 35
Dechert, Bob, 136
Democracy Project (1980), 12, 13
Deng Xiaoping, 130
Denmark, 157
Department of National Defence, 179
*Dictionnaire Classique de la Langue
    Chinoise* (Couvreur), 9–10
Didi Chuxing, 2
Dion, Stéphane, 79, 160
DND, 127

East Asia, 62
Ebola, 52
Egypt, 48
Epp, Weldon, 2
Estonia, 157

Europe, 38, 207, 223, 229
European Union, 13–14, 157, 220

Fadden, Richard, 80, 120, 180
Fahmy, Mohamed, 48
Falun Gong, 207, 238
Fan Wei, 156
Fast, Ed, 38
fentanyl, 85–7, 215
First Nations, 80
Five Eyes, 149, 154, 211, 219
Foreign Agents Registration Act, 117
Foreign Influence Transparency and Accountability Act (FITAA), 133, 134
Foreign Influence Transparency Scheme Act, 113, 117
Foreign Investment Promotion and Protection Agreement (FIPA), 38, 77
France, 49, 157, 160, 189
Freeland, Chrystia, 91–4
free-trade agreement (FTA), 99
Fuzhou Public Security Bureau, 205–6

G20 summit (Osaka), 202
G20, 29–32
Gang of Four, 8
Garratt, Julia, 20, 46, 50
 imprisonment in China, 141–3
 prison release, 144–7
Garratt, Kevin, 20, 46, 50, 78
 imprisonment in China, 141–3
 prison release, 144–7
Gate of Heavenly Peace, 62
Gaza, 225
Germany, 20, 62, 128, 157, 220
Global Times (newspaper), 150, 238
Global TV, 160–1

Globe and Mail, The (newspaper), 27, 207, 209, 211
Grant, Iain, 172
Great Firewall, 61–2
Great Hall of the People, 52, 104
Great Leap Forward economic campaign, 106
Great Wall, 103
Greenland, 220, 225

Hajdu, Patty, 160, 186
Hangzhou, 80, 82
Harper, Stephen, 27–8, 37, 38–9, 41–3, 45–6
Hawke, Bob, 136–7
Hayek, Friedrich, 58, 60
Hogue, Marie-Josée, 134
Hong Kong, 18, 83, 88, 89–90, 99, 150
Hong Kongers, 90, 119
House of Commons, 26, 117, 118
Hu Jintao, 39, 49, 63
Huangdi (Yellow Emperor), 136
Huawei, 112, 116, 118, 127–8, 149
 ban on, 159, 166, 178
 Beijing's assurance to, 190
 Canada's indecision over, 175–7
 impacts on Canada-China relations, 171–4
 See also Ottawa
Hubei Province, 187, 192
Hussain, Mamnoon, 62

In the Name of the People (TV drama), 205
Indonesia, 185
Institute for Research on Public Policy, 81
International Centre for Human Rights and Democratic Development, 15
International Covenant on Civil and Political Rights, 103, 240

International Refugee Board, 35
Investment Canada Act, 42
Iran, 31, 39, 43, 160, 176, 203
Israel, 48
Italy, 189

Jack Ma, 240
Japan, 20, 62, 185, 223, 226, 234
Japanese Canadians, 133
Jiang Zemin, 63, 136
John Chang, 93
Johnson, Boris, 176
Joly, Mélanie, 221, 223
Jordan, 185

Kenny Chiu, 207
Kovrig, Michael, 20, 116, 124, 148–9, 152–3, 154
    tortures in prison, 162–4, 166
Kuomintang, 62
Kymlicka, Will, 16

Lai Changxing, 33–6, 207
Landbridge Group, 133–4
Latin America, 220
Latvia, 157
le Carré, John 2
Legge, James, 8, 9
Lesage, Jean-Francois, 15–16
Li Keqiang, 46, 52–3, 146
Li Peng, 13, 84
Li Qiang, 232
Li Yuchao, 131
Liberation Day, 227, 229
Lithuania, 157
"little emperors", 68–70
Liu Guangbin, 131
Liu Jianhui, 16–17
Liu Shaoqi, 106

Liu Xia, 93
Liu Xiaobo, 50, 93
Lobby groups, 45
Lockheed Martin F-35 fighter jets, 226
Lu Shaye, 160
Luo Zhaohui, 76

MAGA, 226, 227, 230
"Make China Great Again", 215
Malaysia, 62
Mao Zedong, 3, 8, 65, 69, 84, 200
Mar-a-Lago, 220
Massot, Pascale, 160
Matas, David, 35
McCallum, John, 92–3, 150, 154, 161, 200, 203
McMaster, H.R., 190
Meng Wanzhou, 113, 116, 150, 162–4, 175–6, 203
    arrest of, 124, 148–9, 165
Merkel, Angela, 173
#MeToo protesters, 131
Middle East, 48
Ministry of State Security (MSS), 135–6
Montreal, 112
Moscow, 213, 219
Muddy Waters, 40
Mugabe, Robert, 31, 66
Mulroney, David, 210
Munich, 220
Myanmar, 26

NAFTA, 91, 108, 199
Nash, Knowlton, 12
National Health Commission (China), 192
National People's Congress, 51, 53, 103, 105, 231
National Research Council (Canada), 142, 145

NATO, 157, 179, 225, 228
Natural Sciences and Engineering Research Council, 122
NDP, 26
Netherlands, 16, 20, 157
New Zealand, 99, 107, 177
Nexen, 42–3, 65, 76
NGOs, 14
North America, 222
North Korea, 26, 31–2, 43, 62, 143, 203
North Korean Christians, 142, 145
Northern Fleet, 213
Northern Gateway pipeline, 76, 80
NSICOP, 136
Nuctech, 216

Oliphant, Robert, 119
Ontario, 233
Opium War, 86, 95
Osborne, George, 64
Ottawa, 19, 26–7, 87, 111–13, 116, 133
    decision on Huawei, 159–61, 216
    defence funding announcements, 213
    faced pressure to release Meng, 203
    key steps to protect Canada's sovereignty, 209–11
    need for program fundings, 124
    new approach to China, 199–201
    reconsidering Canada's relations with China, 186
    resolution on Chinese EVs, 222

Pakistan, 110
Panama, 225
Parliamentary Foreign Affairs Committee, 14
Peking Review (magazine), 7
Pelosi, Nancy, 176

Pentagon, 231
Philippines, 62
PMO, 94, 104
Political and Legal Affairs Commissions, 222–3
Port Darwin, 134
Portugal, 185
"post-Tiananmen bargain", 130
Putin, Vladimir, 62, 126–7, 179

Qin Gang, 131
"Quadrilateral Security Dialogue", 123, 125
Quentin Huang, 180

Radio Free Asia, 225
Rand Corporation, 231
Randt, Clark, 14–15
RCMP, 119, 127, 137, 179, 206, 211
Regina, 235
Reinhart, Kevin, 76
Remembrance Day ceremonies, 44
Robb, Andrew, 133–4
Rome, 107
Royal Society of Canada, 12
Royal United Services Institute (RUSI), 115
Rubio, Marco, 224
Rudd, Kevin, 116
Russia, 101, 110, 128, 160, 214, 226
    attack on Ukraine, 178
    joint military exercises with China, 213
Russians, 97, 100, 126

Safeguard Defenders, 205, 206–7
SARS, 186, 189, 192
Saskatchewan, 233, 235
Sasktel, 172
Saudi Arabia, 112, 160
Schellenberg, Lloyd, 156

Schellenberg, Robert, 148
Shanghai Airport, 114–15
Shanghai, 1–2, 3, 5, 33
Shi Rong, 136
Shore, Michel, 35
shuanggui, 83
Sick Kids Hospital, 17
Singh, Harjit, 186
South America, 110, 201
South Asia, 110
South China Post (newspaper), 115
South China Sea, 62, 80, 110, 212, 216, 220
    Chinese expansion, 65, 83, 99, 115, 150
South Korea, 62, 99–100, 185, 223
Spain, 157, 189
Spavor, Michael, 20, 113, 116, 124, 148–9, 152–3
    tortures in prison, 162–4, 166
Sri Lanka, 110
Stevens, Geoffrey, 12
stock market
    crisis, 54–6
Su Bin, 145–6
Sudan, 26, 31, 39, 43
Sun Zhengcai, 106
Sweden, 20

Taiwan Strait, 220
Taiwan, 7, 18, 20, 127, 193
    China's claim over, 234–5
    COVID-19 outbreak, 192
Tang Dynasty, 227
Tao Liming, 1–2
Taoism, 3, 8
Telus, 172, 175
Third World, 49, 65, 97, 128
Three Gorges Dam, 102

Tiananmen Square, 61, 62, 65, 90
    massacre, 11, 18–19
Tianjin, 63
Tibet, 43, 150, 238
Tibetans, 16, 43, 112, 119, 157, 207
Toronto Star (newspaper), 17–18
Toronto, 112, 135–6, 206
TP-Link routers, 216
Treaty of Nanking (1842), 86
Treaty of Versailles (1919), 3
Trudeau, Justin, 65, 76–7, 92, 108, 125, 199
    support for Barton, 161
    visit to China, 82–3, 98
    Wang Yi and, 146
Trudeau, Pierre, 65, 66, 83–4, 200
Trump, Donald, 96, 176, 199, 218–20
    aid to Xi Jinping, 224–6
    met with Xi Jinping, 202–4
    trade dispute with China, 108–10
Tsang, Steve, 188–9
Tsinghua University, 82
Turkic Muslims, 118, 157

Uber, 2
Ukraine, 126, 128, 178, 181, 220
UN Convention on the Law of the Sea, 83
UN Genocide Convention, 118
UN International Covenant on Civil and Political Rights, 200
UN Security Council, 31
United Front Work Department (UFWD), 107, 121
United Kingdom, 157, 211
United Nations, 13–14, 123, 213, 225, 234, 240
United States, 20, 49, 99–100, 150, 185
    investigation on COVID-19 pandemic, 190
    relations between Canada and, 218–20

rivalry between China and, 156
trade dispute with China, 108–10
Xi Jinping's predictions on, 239
University of Alberta, 121
University of British Columbia, 121
Uyghur Muslims, 124
Uyghur Rights Advocacy Project, 238
Uyghurs, 43, 150, 154, 167, 189, 202–3

Vancouver, 112, 207
Venezuela, 43, 101, 112
Venezuelans, 97
Voice of America, 225

Wai Young, 216
Wang Huning, 232
Wang Qishan, 105
Wang Wenbin, 115
Wang Yi, 79, 91–2, 93, 146
Wang Zhaojun, 11
Wang Zhemin, 2
Warsaw Pact, 126
Washington, 14, 38, 100, 108–9, 176, 214
WeChat, 5
Wen Jiabao, 173
WikiLeaks, 14
Wind, 172
World Bank, 102
World Health Assembly, 193
World Health Organization (WHO), 189, 192–3
World Military Games, 189
World Trade Organization, 30, 66, 109, 115, 123, 226
World War II, 62, 133, 221
WTO, 99, 228, 240
Wu Guohua, 131
Wuhan, 185–7, 191–2

Xi Jinping, 3, 16, 19–20, 50
anti-corruption campaign, 59
dictatorship, 231–3
foreign-policy vision, 225
met with Trump, 202–4
national restoration plan, 95–7
political damage, 130–1
visit to Britain, 64
visit to Hong Kong, 88
See also Trump, Donald
Xiamen, 35
Xiao Baolong, 45–6
Xinhua news agency, 91, 105
Xinjiang, 43, 134, 167, 238, 240
Xu Zhongbo, 131

Yalu River, 141–2, 145
Yan Beiming, 3

Zhang Dejiang, 90
Zhang Zhenzhong, 131
Zhao Lijian, 188, 189
Zhao Ziyang, 65
Zhou Enlai, 65, 84, 106
Zimbabwe, 26, 43, 83
Zuma, Jacob, 62